Practicing What You Preach

Practicing What You Preach

Self-Care for Helping Professionals

Jeffrey A. Kottler, Ph.D.

cognella®
SAN DIEGO

Bassim Hamadeh, CEO and Publisher
Amy Smith, Senior Project Editor
Casey Hands, Production Editor
Jess Estrella, Senior Graphic Designer
Stephanie Kohl, Licensing Coordinator
Natalie Piccotti, Director of Marketing
Kassie Graves, Vice President of Editorial
Jamie Giganti, Director of Academic Publishing

3970 Sorrento Valley Blvd., Ste. 500, San Diego, CA 92121

Brief Contents

Detailed Contents

Preface

Throughout my long career as a teacher, counselor, psychologist, administrator, and social justice advocate, I have suffered every possible kind of job-related stress. I've been haunted by the tragic stories of a few clients, irrevocably traumatized by things I've witnessed when working in earthquake- and flood-ravaged countries, subjected to toxic work cultures and abuse by supervisors, and I'm still licking my wounds from career disappointments, session failures, misguided choices, and almost five decades of exposure to some of the most difficult and annoying people I've ever known. I've been cheated by clients, lied to by others, manipulated and stalked, shamed and attacked. I've been subjected to far worse by a few colleagues over the years who seemed more disturbed and dangerous than any of the people I've treated in consultations.

I've experienced almost every conceivable manifestation of occupational stress in all their various forms, including countertransference, projective identification, compassion fatigue, primary and secondary trauma, and burnout. I've quit more jobs than I can remember, each time vowing I will never again subject myself to such misery and lack of support. I've been in and out of more forms of supervision and therapy than I can easily recall. I've had more than my fair share of nightmares and insomnia. I've written more books about the doubts, and uncertainties, and tribulations of therapy practice than anyone else alive. And I've failed at more different kinds of self-care strategies than I can possibly name. I guess you could say I'm an expert on the unnecessary burdens and failed practices of therapists trying to take care of themselves as well as their clients. I can also say, with considerable pride, that I've learned over time to develop remarkable resilience and the ability to recover from life's (and work's) challenges and disappointments, maintaining tremendous passion, joy, and enthusiasm for my devotion to helping others in spite of the stressors.

Outside of the psychotherapy world, stress has become the focal point of discomfort, dissatisfaction, even longevity among the general population. Given the work and lifestyle demands of professional helpers and healers, the incidence of emotional difficulties as a result of work responsibilities is far greater. We are at greater risk for stress disorders, plus the additional wear and tear on our psyche from vicarious and secondary trauma. Burnout affects somewhere between half to three-quarters of all practitioners at some point in their careers. Some professionals never quite recover.

As a result of this predicament, self-care has become an obsession. Americans spend an average of one-quarter of their disposable income on nonessential, material possessions, luxury items, and services designed to make themselves feel better. (Younger people spend up to one-third of their disposable income on self-care items.) People feel they deserve such things because they work so hard and deal with so much stress in their lives, yet they also feel a certain amount of guilt over the self-indulgences. They view this behavior less as a form of pampering than as a means by which to tolerate their daily pressures.

The subject of self-care has become so popular that it has eclipsed almost everything else in the popularity of self-help books and social media posts. During times of economic uncertainty, global crises, traumatic events, and pandemics, self-care becomes the single most critical topic of discussion. There is no time when this has been more the case.

People routinely share with the world images of themselves supposedly engaged in restorative activities—gallivanting on a beach, huddling with friends in a selfie pose, or pretending to enjoy their isolation. There are more books published on self-care than any other topic, so much so that Amazon has sub-divided the genre into two dozen different categories, including diet, exercise, mindfulness, time management, and personal transformation, to mention a few. Then there are all the books like this one directed to professionals in order to help us to recover from the strains and demands of our jobs, or to supposedly prevent such difficulties by adopting one of the recommended strategies. Many of them offer simplistic advice: All we have to do is practice mindfulness every day, repeat positive affirmations, or perhaps join a gym or commit to daily walks. It is the same well-intended but relatively ineffective admonishments we may offer to our own clients—which hardly ever stick over time.

Although we will review many of the strategies and techniques that are known to improve daily functioning and help us recover from the daily stress-ors of our jobs, self-care is really more about an internalized commitment. It is just as futile reducing the process to a few simple habits as it is telling our depressed or anxious clients that all they have to do is light a scented candle and take a warm bath. That is certainly a nice, relaxing way to spend time, but it doesn't really address the underlying toxic and soul-crushing influences that wear us down.

Self-care is actually a full-time job, not just an occasional reminder that it's time to take a break or a deep breath. Given that the "self" is the primary means by which we relate to others, regardless of our specialty and discipline, it is imper-ative that it is functioning optimally, relatively free from distress, distractions, and bias. During those times when we might feel dispirited or stressed, it takes a *lot* more than registering for a yoga or spin class to turn things around. Of course, every little bit helps but, ultimately, permanent relief and rejuvenation occurs only after truly addressing the source of the misery, whether that is a dysfunctional organizational climate, a neglectful or abusive supervisor, schedule overload, unresolved personal issues, interpersonal conflicts, or an unhealthy lifestyle. There are often big issues involved, not just a few little adjustments that are supposed to turn things around. In some ways, taking on some new self-care practices can feel like just another burden, something else added to your schedule that either takes up limited time or makes you feel even more guilty and helpless when you don't get around to it.

Despite the differences in our disciplines, theoretical allegiances, work settings, and clientele, there are several fairly universal features that are part of almost every clinician's experience that make us especially vulnerable to chronic stress. Our best efforts directed toward taking better care of ourselves often fail to have much lasting impact once we lose much of our passion, motivation, energy, and creativity, which are all exhaustible resources.

This book is primarily designed as a resource for classes in social work, counseling, family therapy, psychology, human services, health professions, and other related fields, as well as a guide for practitioners. Early career clinicians are especially vulnerable to the challenges of therapeutic practice, often because of unrealistic expectations for what is possible, limited experience and resources to deal with adversity, and an inability to process disappointments, mistakes, and failures constructively.

It is one of the frustrating realities and miscalculations of our work that the attempt to take care of ourselves, as well as to serve others, is often made considerably more challenging by the added burden and obligations of sticking with some rigid program that just seems to add additional pressures and feelings of discouragement. This is why most self-care strategies not only don't work very well, but can actually lead to even greater frustration and increased stress. And yet, there are indeed some approaches and attitudes, many of which we teach to others, that do produce enduring changes and help us to better metabolize the difficult things we are required to face.

There has been considerable research on occupational stress and burnout in the last decades, driven, in part, by lost productivity, absenteeism, health complaints, addictions, and morale problems on the job. It is well known that once people reach a state of emotional exhaustion and depletion it is often too late to pull out of a tailspin, no matter how many facials, massages, shopping sprees, or quick fixes are attempted to manage the chronic stress. In this book, we review the nature and manifestations of acute and chronic compassion fatigue, vicarious trauma, and related conditions, examining the origins of these difficulties. We examine why self-care usually does not work very well, for very long, and why it is so difficult to begin and maintain more healthy habits. In many cases, it is the very attempt to address the problems that ends up creating new and different challenges. It is clear that if we wish to have much lasting impact with our clients, much less maintain our own sense of efficacy with them, we must develop self-care strategies that serve and support us throughout our lifetimes, all designed to reduce the burdens of our work. It is imperative that we are able—and willing—to practice with ourselves what we preach to others.

Jeffrey Kottler
Houston, Texas

CHAPTER 1

Congruence, Authenticity, and Hypocrisy

It is late at night and I cannot sleep. Every time I close my eyes, I see before me a scene in which I stand helpless, mute, unable to express myself. I think of several things I could have said, brilliant responses that would have moved my adversary to tears, speechlessness, or, better yet, recognition that I am right and he is wrong.

In my dreams I can say these things, but I cannot seem to mobilize such persuasive arguments in the midst of real conflicts. "Why must he treat me this way?" I beseech the sandman, who will not release me from consciousness. "Why will he not be more reasonable, more cooperative, *more like me*?"

My breathing slows. I finally find a comfortable position. The demons are buried in sand and I am floating away. Suddenly, my eyes pop open once again. "Now, wait a minute," I remind myself. "Did he really mean it when he said ... ?" "Next time he does that I am going to ... " Indignation. Rage. Shame. Frustration. Fear. Tension. Uncertainty. Blame. No wonder I can't sleep.

My work within this organization had begun to feel like a prison sentence. All my clients started to sound the same to me. I had even started thinking about a great new book idea called "Clients From Hell," in which each chapter would be devoted to a different kind of client who was driving me crazy. You know, the one who talks and never listens, or the one who just refused to speak at all. There would be chapters on the rageful client who goes off on rants blaming me for everything wrong in his life. Then there's the completely unresponsive client, a victim of serial abuse and neglect, whose story breaks my heart and makes me feel completely helpless because there's nothing I seem to be able to do for her. The list goes on and on. But it wasn't my clients who were the main source of misery; it was a few of my colleagues who were mean-spirited, vindictive, and hurtful.

Whether it was the result of compassion fatigue, vicarious trauma, burnout, or my own lingering traumatic experiences from the past, what seemed clear was that I was not enjoying my work—or my life—very much. I felt stale and bored, seeming to have the same conversations over and over again. I'd look at my schedule and start to feel a sense of dread, if not panic, when I'd see a few particular names. I tried to think of any legitimate excuse to avoid staff meetings, which left me wrung out and emotionally depleted. People would attack one another, call each other names, mostly because we were competing for limited resources but also because some of them were just downright mean-spirited and insecure. It was their hypocrisy that bothered me most, that these were professionals who were supposed to demonstrate caring, compassion, and good cheer for all and yet some of them were just grumpy and annoying.

I took up the mission of self-care, picked up the length and speed of my morning runs, attended classes in Tai Chi, tried to diversify my life, planned escapist adventures, anything to drown out the emptiness and dissatisfaction I felt going into work. I started looking for other jobs but this sort of thing had happened previously, so it got me wondering what I was doing (or not doing) to get myself back into this period of disillusionment. Was this just an inevitable stage that occurs after a while? Was I creating this situation thorough my own neglect and self-righteousness? These were the sorts of questions that led me to consider the ways I organize my life, not to mention the sort of negative attitudes that seemed to creep in when I was being lazy or complacent. Worse of all, I felt like such a hypocrite for telling my students, clients, and supervisees how critical it is to not settle for mediocrity, to take constructive risks, and to accept personal responsibility for one's troubles and dissatisfactions instead of blaming others.

Legacy of Hypocrisy

I know I am hardly the only therapist or helping professional who sometimes neglects to take care of himself and fails to model those practices that I advocate for others. Some of our most prominent figures attained such notoriety because of their workaholism and single-minded drive toward achievement. Albert Ellis famously boasted of his 16-hour workdays to pack in all the things he wished to accomplish, often to the neglect of his personal life. Carl Rogers (1995, p. 80), one of the grandparents of humanism and relational therapy, once admitted, "I have always been better at caring for and looking after others than I have been at caring for myself. But in later years, I have made progress." Indeed, it wasn't until well into his seventies that he recovered from alcoholism, chronic depression, and feelings of isolation. Likewise, Irvin Yalom (2002, p. 252) remarked how our work can completely take over our lives: "At the end of our workday, having given so much of ourselves, we feel drained of desire for more relationship."

Resolving relational conflicts is one of those tasks that is supposed to be the lifeblood of therapeutic work. We are experts in human relationships and are often called upon to resolve disputes for a living. We mediate conflicts, cool down hostilities between spouses, business partners, siblings, parents and children. We spend much of our lives acting as referees between warring family members, settling long-standing arguments, and dealing with conflicts that often seem intractable and, at times, even hopeless. Given sufficient time, as well as commitment on the part of our clients, we are often able to help people to reconcile their differences, set aside their resentments, and come to a deeper appreciation for one another's positions.

Yet with all our training and experience, all the hours we log helping other people work through their interpersonal struggles, we hardly remain immune from such conflicts ourselves. I am supposedly an expert in helping people sort out their difficulties, so it is with particular reluctance that I admit the extent to which I have allowed myself to become deeply troubled about relationships that have caused me great anguish and frustration. Furthermore, I cannot think of a time when this has not been the case. It seems that almost everyone loses sleep over relationships in conflict.

Like most therapists, I have been down this road with enough people—children fighting with their parents; siblings who will not speak to one another; spouses on the verge of divorce; friends estranged from one another; people in conflict with supervisors, co-workers, ex-spouses, neighbors—to know that there are few undertakings as difficult as coming to terms with conflict, both with our clients and within ourselves.

I have long been both fascinated and disturbed by the degree of hypocrisy operating in our profession (or in any profession) in which we preach things to our clients that we can't (or won't) do in our own lives. We tell people that they should let go of things they can't control, yet are not able to do so ourselves. We give pep talks about the importance of creating more intimacy in relationships and all the while we don't make this much of a priority in our own lives. We admonish clients to avoid allowing antagonists to live "rent free" in their heads yet struggle with our own demons who haunt us at night—or throughout the day. We advocate compassion, empathy, and the practice of kindness, even demonstrate them consistently in sessions while the meter is running, yet we can become as belligerent, insensitive, and hostile as anyone else when operating in the world outside our domain. If anything, we may even be more prone to narcissism and self-centeredness because of the ways we are worshipped and deified by clients who so admire our composure and wisdom (Clark, 1991; Welt & Herron, 1990). We may also be vulnerable to a whole array of personal conflicts with family, friends, and colleagues, precisely because we are used to being in charge of relationships.

Helping professionals are often remarkably stubborn when faced with the prospect of needing help themselves. After trying—and failing—repeatedly with self-care strategies, two-thirds of practicing psychologists who were surveyed reported that although they were significantly distressed because of personal losses, vicarious trauma, compassion fatigue, and negative countertransference reactions, they still refused to consult with a therapist (Dattilio, 2015; Walsh, 2011). A similar trajectory of neglect occurs within the wider medical community. Although fully 98% of practicing physicians, along with 88% of their patients, believe that self-care programs should be an essential component of all healthcare, half of doctors claim that people just aren't interested in even discussing the possibilities. Virtually all patients say that, at one time or another, they have tried self-care for their various maladies, but the commitment doesn't stick very long; they claim that they don't have the time, resources, or financial ability to continue their plans. Among the physicians themselves, although stress and burnout sometimes feel out of control, the vast majority say that the demands of their jobs prevent them from making the time to take care of their own health and welfare (Jonas, 2019). This disconnection between what healthcare providers say is important for others and what they are actually willing to do for themselves is indefensible.

Neglect of Self-Care

Those of us in the business of helping others, whether in the role of educators, counselors, psychotherapists, health professionals, or leaders, strive to provide support and care for others. We apply methods, teach strategies, introduce pro-cedures, or choose interventions that are specifically designed to reduce suffering and promote greater life satisfaction and well-being. We scold and cajole our clients, students, patients, or followers into practicing healthy lifestyle habits. We assign homework that fosters cognitive and intellectual development. We recommend habits that balance work with time for recovery. We prescribe tasks that lead to higher functioning. We tell almost everyone how important it is to take better care of themselves. Take up an exercise program. Join a gym. Eat brown rice. Meditate or practice mindfulness. Take naps. Stop smoking, vaping, and overeating. Refrain from excessive indulgences. Prioritize family and friends. Cut down on work hours. Reduce screen time. Limit time on mobile devices. Each of us has a list of things that we believe are good for people. And because we are experienced and accomplished in our fields, we rely on solid research and wisdom to support this evidence-based advice.

What, then, are we doing for ourselves?

The truth is that many of us who take care of others are not so good at taking care of ourselves. Burnout, stress, compassion fatigue, and vicarious trauma have never been higher among those of us who help others for a living. One half of all practicing physicians and one third of nurses report major symptoms of burn-out or stress-related disorders (Reith, 2018). During times of crises, catastrophic events, and pandemics almost everyone feels out of control in some way. Social workers, psychologists, and counselors report significant difficulties in their daily functioning as a result of accumulated stress and professional responsibilities (Simionato & Simpson, 2018). Among teachers, burnout has been described as rising to epidemic proportions, affecting three quarters of those surveyed, resulting in sleep and appetite disturbances, depression, chronic anxiety, and a host of stress-related symptoms like headaches, dizziness, and chest pain (Anthony, 2019). It would thus appear that all our knowledge, training, skills, and commitment to serve others is not being applied very consistently and diligently to ourselves!

This is all the more surprising considering that a significant part of our jobs involves helping people adjust to the unrelenting pressures of their work and lives. Recent surveys have confirmed what we already know—that 96% of managers and supervisors report that their employees are overwhelmed and suffering from acute burnout and neglect of self-care, and almost one third are barely functional because of extreme symptoms of depletion and exhaustion (Schneider, 2019b).

Whether in the classroom, clinic, or office, we are supposed experts on teaching others to take care of themselves, to metabolize stress and life challenges in effective ways. We admonish our students or clients to develop sound and healthy habits—and stick with them consistently—all the while we languish in our own complacency, working excessive hours and neglecting many of the same priorities we recommend for others. Does this imply we don't really believe in what we offer to others, or rather that we are simply hypocrites who don't practice what we preach?

Wounded Healers

It's interesting to consider why we chose helping professions for our life's work in the first place. Is it because we wanted an excuse to deal with our own personal struggles, or rather is it the demanding work itself that pushes us to a breaking point? There's little doubt that we are exposed to people on a daily basis who are among the most difficult, annoying, troubled, conflicted, impulsive, complaining individuals on the planet, often suffering from a lifetime of trauma and disappointments. We listen to their stories and can't help but take them on board. At times it feels like their symptoms might be contagious.

Many of the most luminary historical figures in mental health were barely functional themselves. Sigmund Freud had an assortment of different emotional maladies, including blackouts, agoraphobia, cocaine addiction, and superstitious behavior related to numbers. (He was convinced he would die at 62.) He was prone to clearly self-destructive behavior, insisting on continuing to smoke cigars even after he was in agonizing pain from cancer of the mouth and jaw.

William James, the very first psychologist, dealt with chronic depression. Carl Rogers never felt understood throughout his life, struggling with depression and alcoholism. Lawrence Kohlberg researched stages of moral development, fascinated with the higher order of personal choice that guides behavior. After developing health problems, he committed suicide by walking into the Atlantic Ocean. Psychiatrist R. D. Laing glorified and celebrated mental illness as another form of creativity and individuality, all the while slowly falling apart in his own mental deterioration. Marsha Linehan, creator of a therapeutic approach to treat borderline personality disorder, suffers from this same condition. We know such difficulties among professionals are not exactly rare considering that two-thirds of psychologists have reported serious depression and one-third have admitted suicidal ideation. Among psychiatrists, one-third admitted to symptoms of mental illness at one time or another, a condition that many attempted to hide from others (Yasgur, 2019).

In one study of mental health workers, although all of those who were interviewed reported symptoms of stress, vicarious trauma, or secondary traumatic stress at one time or another, none of them admitted they practiced self-care on a daily basis (Sawicki, 2019). They described their jobs as "intense, demanding, stressful, draining, hard, frustrating, difficult, and challenging," yet in spite of their symptoms, "stress, anxiety, feelings of inadequacy, recurring thoughts, sleeplessness, nightmares, hyper-vigilance, heart palpitations, panic, breathing difficulty, migraines, headaches, and appetite issues," not one of them sought help from either medical professionals or supervisors (p. 246). They all felt a certain amount of shame related to their difficulties, leading them to keep their problems to themselves and try to deal with the issues on their own without organizational support.

Although this subject is most often discussed as merely a desirable priority for helping professionals, there are some who consider it an ethical imperative (Dalphon, 2019; Newell & Nelson-Gardell, 2014). After all, we use the "self" as the primary instrument for assessment, diagnosis, and treatment; if the self is neglected, it will likely affect professional effectiveness in a number of significant ways—distorting judgment, compromising clarity and objectivity, eroding patience and tolerance, taking shortcuts to save limited time and energy.

Hypocrisy, Congruence, and Practicing What We Preach

Almost 30 years ago I wrote an article disclosing an awareness of my own hypocrisy with respect to inconsistencies between my talk and my actions (Kottler, 1992b). I had just given a lecture to a group of graduate students in counseling about the critical importance of compassion and caring in all our daily interactions, not just when the meter was running in sessions with clients. I was passionate and absolute in my pronouncements, urging, if not demanding, that we exude empathy and respect toward others.

During a break, a student approached me to challenge a marginal grade I had awarded his mid-term assignment. He was wanting to better understand the reasoning behind my decision, which didn't make sense to him. I immediately became defensive at his questioning my judgment, and when he persisted, I became even more strident. I could see nervous, uncomfortable glances from the other students who overheard the conversation, but they quickly averted their eyes. Upon reflection, I realized that during this encounter I had lapsed into authoritarian mode and was hardly a picture of composure and understanding. But what struck me the most is that the other students observing the conflict didn't seem particularly surprised by this type of response from one of their professors. It was as if this was particularly expected and normal—that we may advocate one thing for them, but because we hold the power, we are permitted to behave quite differently, even if it directly contradicts the things that we say are so important. Throughout my own experience as a student, I noticed over and over again how often my instructors and supervisors seemed to be the antithesis of the lessons and themes they introduced. Many of them hadn't actually practiced their craft in decades. Others seemed absolutely clueless about what others really thought about them—or they just didn't seem to care. They'd drone on and on about issues and values that they could not, or would not, demonstrate in their own behavior.

This has led to a journey spanning many decades in which I continually question the ways that I, and others in positions of leadership, power, and control, fail to practice what we preach. Given the current political/social climate in our country, and around the world, it has now become even more accepted that politicians, corporate executives, health professionals, and others in power can engage in blatantly hypocritical behavior without serious consequences, eroding the very foundations of sanctioned moral codes. Political or business leaders can proclaim ridiculous lies without consequences. They can engage in exploitative behavior, pad their own bank accounts, or break the same rules they demand for others, and do so with a self-righteous grin on their faces.

More recently, I've found that with age and experience I've learned to be more forgiving, viewing the striving for congruence as the ultimate in self-care (Neace & Kottler, 2017). I've devoted much of my personal and professional growth over the years to learning to live with imperfections and never feeling good enough (Kottler & Blau, 1989; Kottler & Carlson, 2002; Kottler, 2018). It is a reality of our work that we will never really know enough, or be able to function at the optimal level that we prefer.

Quite a few philosophers throughout the ages have taken indignant issue with hypocrisy. The word is derived from the Greek, referring to a fraudulent and deceptive appearance. Martin (2014) reviews some of the historical thoughts on the matter. Theophrastus attacked this trait as a major vice. Cicero considered it a disqualifier of true friendship. During more recent times, Hannah Arendt (1963) considered it to be the "vice of all vices" because it completely erodes integrity, "rotten to the core."

By contrast, the congruence between espoused beliefs and subsequent actions has been characterized as a sign of nobility. One reason why this consistency might be so rare is the reality that we are much better at deceiving ourselves than we are fooling others. That is precisely what allows us to continue to engage in such inconsistent behavior which, at times, is highly functional in that it allows us to partition our beliefs according to particular needs and context. It is thus a mindset that is both desirable and also useful from an evolutionary perspective. It saves energy and allows people to get away with things that would ordinarily be prohibited. One annoying side effect, however, is that we have to manufacture excuses to justify the actions.

Perhaps this helps explain how it is possible that (a) one quarter of Florida police officers routinely speed in excess of 100 miles per hour when they are off duty, (b) 40% of physicians are significantly overweight, (c) ethics professors are no more moral in their daily behavior than the general population, or (d) most of those who shoplift from stores are the employees (Green, 2015). In addition, it was discovered some time ago that 60% of practicing counselors continue to see clients when they are significantly distressed themselves (Pope, Tabachnick, & Keith-Spiegel, 1987).

In spite of ethical philosophers and religious scholars proclaiming the importance of universal love and kindness, there have been millions of occupants on this planet killed in the name of God because their views differ from those in power. "How many Christians actually turn the other cheek?" Harari (2018, p. 58) asks. "How many Buddhists actually rise above egoistic obsessions, and how many Jews actually love their neighbors as themselves?" In spite of our best intentions, we are ruled by instinctual emotions that are driven by fear, anger, anxiety, and uncertainty. It is precisely these feelings that account for the sort of impulsive, distracted behavior that results in more than a million traffic deaths each year, double the number caused by war, violence, crime, and terrorism.

Cultural Contexts

When professionals fail to invest in their own self-care consistently, it also has negative consequences for their patients, clients, and students (Mills & Chapman, 2016). Within the medical profession, doctors have traditionally displayed overt signs of personal neglect and burnout as a kind of badge of honor, demonstrating their sacrifices and commitment to the profession. As residents they were required to work under brutal conditions of sleep deprivation and 36-hour shifts, not to mention crushing debt from medical school. After such inhumane working conditions, and the influence of medical culture, many doctors just continue the excessive hours once they are in practice.

McKinnon (1991) makes a clear distinction between someone who is dishonest about intentions to create a favorable impression versus the sort of hypocrisy that undermines the system of morality. If a king, president, CEO, psychotherapist, physician, teacher, or clergy member preaches to their constituents, employees, clients, students, patients, or congregation that certain behaviors are forbidden or wrong, and then secretly (or openly) engages in those actions, the whole structure falls apart. Or at least that's the dominant idea.

There are more than subtle differences between mere self-deception and true hypocrisy. In the case of lying to oneself, it could be involuntary, beyond awareness, and a kind of defense mechanism against perceived threats, real or imagined. Hypocrisy, on the other hand, is purposely designed to be deceptive and manipulate others for personal gain.

It's also interesting to consider the ways that hypocrisy is culturally contextual, pretty much like any other aspect of behavior. It turns out, for example, that people in Japan, India, or Indonesia react quite differently and more mildly to inconsistencies between espoused beliefs and subsequent actions (Effron et al., 2018). In Western cultures, such hypocrisy is often judged harshly but there are many different kinds of such behavior:

- saying one thing but doing another
- failure to demonstrate in behavior the values and priorities advocated for others
- excusing oneself from actions that are condemned in others
- pretending to be someone or something you are not (honest, transparent, fair, authentic)
- deceptive behavior to mask true beliefs for personal gain
- claiming knowledge that one actually lacks

Some types of hypocrisy are tolerated, if not indulged and accepted, more than others, depending on cultural norms and practices. There is often a distinction made between so-called "word-deed misalignment" and the kind of moral breach evident in deliberate deception for personal gain. From an evolutionary perspective, the latter is potentially catastrophic when the functioning and survival of the community depends on mutual trust and the avoidance of exploitation.

Guarded Prognosis

There are tens of thousands of books on the subject of self-care, the most popular genre of all when you add into the mix all the books on diets, exercise, mindfulness, self-esteem, recovery, resilience, happiness, life satisfaction, and well-being. In spite of all these options, the sad irony is that hardly any of these programs appear to work very well for very long. The most compelling argument for this statement is that 70% of those with gym or fitness memberships *never* use the services they pay for (averaging $60 *every* month!). Just think about that as a business model—convincing people to pay for something that they won't ever use! When members are questioned as to why they waste their money they often report that they fully *intend* to visit the facilities at some point—once they have the time to do so. Essentially they are renting some guilt appeasement.

Given that the vast majority of Americans are significantly overweight, it is not surprising that one popular self-care plan relates directly to dieting. People feel that if only they could lose an extra 10 (20, or 30) pounds, they'd feel so much better about themselves, their body image, and their ultimate health. There are all kinds of compelling reasons for such a choice, considering how carrying extra weight leads to an assortment of problems, from lower back pain, strokes, and heart attacks to reduced life expectancy. In spite of the importance of such an effort, the passionate commitments that people make to this declaration, they will try more than a half dozen different diet plans without lasting success. Every time some new quick fix weight-loss or exercise program hits the market it is seen as the panacea for all that ails us. Likewise, the popularity of the latest mindfulness practice, hot yoga, meditation, or cannabis-infused treats, is based on the promise that they will take the edge off the chronic stress in our lives.

The Limits of Self-Care

We often talk about self-care as if it is the solution to all our problems. We should know better than most others that there are clear limits to what we can do for ourselves, whether addressing medical complaints, emotional difficulties, or the accumulation of new skills or knowledge. Otherwise, why would teachers, doctors, counselors, psychotherapists, accountants, and lawyers exist in the first place?

Self-help books may be interesting, if not enlightening, but their enduring impact is pitiful. If self-help, self-care, and diet books really worked all that well, why would we need so many of them? The self-improvement market is a $15 billion industry. People flock to motivational talks, personal growth semi-nars, miracle drugs, quick fixes, and purchase books that are supposed to make us happier and eliminate stress. As mentioned in the introduction, the self-help genre is so popular these days that there are dozens of different categories, all of which imply that self-care is within each of our capabilities—if only we get the right resource. My favorite example of the self-help options is a book entitled *Faking It: How to Seem Like a Better Person Without Actually Improving Yourself*.

In another popular but misguided attempt to take better care of ourselves, we measure everything and anything related to the self—watches, 3D accelerometers,

GPS transceivers, biometric sensors, mobile devices, and implants all provide a barrage of information every moment about your habits, behavior, diet, heart rate, blood pressure, sleep cycle, oxygen and blood levels, and precise location in time and space. It's as if once we have all this data on every aspect of our being, somehow that means we will do something meaningful with the information. It's not like this ever worked very well in the past, as anyone on a diet knows after weighing themselves on a scale. In defending these latest monitors, including earbuds that will automatically measure biometric indices or microscopic sensors that measure minute changes in physiology, it is believed that all this self-directed technology that helps us know ourselves better will lead to lifestyle changes and better self-care efforts. That's great in theory, but the reality is that people realize all kinds of things about themselves that are unhealthy or self-destructive and yet it doesn't necessarily stop them from continuing these habits. Inscribed on the packages of cigarettes for decades has been a warning that the contents will kill you, but it doesn't stop many smokers from continuing to indulge in the habit.

Self-care is really about prevention, structuring certain nonnegotiable habits and practices in our daily life so that stress symptoms or emotional fatigue never reach the point where they feel out of control. Once burnout kicks in, it's often far too late to fix things on our own. That's why supervision, peer support, and personal therapy are so critical during such times to help us gain a better (or different) perspective and to make the necessary, urgent adjustments (or radical transformations) that are so clearly indicated.

We are blamed, or blame ourselves, for the choices, lifestyle preferences, and personal deficiencies that lead to our misery and dissatisfactions. We are repeatedly told that if only we changed our diets, exercised more, became more mindful, all would be well. Yet there are social, economic, political, cultural, and environmental factors that have such a strong influence on our behavior and subsequent reactions. There is, thus, some question as to whether the whole idea of "stress" as a phenomena really exists in the ways we normally think about it. Furthermore, this supposition that all our reactions to adversity exist within a social context implies that *self*-care is futile without exploring the underlying roots.

Becker (2013) mentions all the ways we are bombarded with terrifying stories about what stress is doing to our bodies, our minds, job performance, and relationships, our very sense of well-being. It has even been called the "Black Death," likened to the plague that killed 25 million people and considered responsible for more deaths than strokes, heart attacks, or cancer. As much anxiety, fear, illness, and death that was caused by a more recent pandemic, the health consequences still pale compared to the effects of chronic stress. Becker, therefore, makes the case that stress is not only a metaphor, but an idea, not just a condition. There have been other times in history when stress as an idea didn't even yet exist.

It was Hans Selye, the "inventor" of stress as we now conceive it, who once remarked that "one cannot be cured of stress, but can only learn to enjoy it." He made his remarkable discovery, which he later called the "general adaptation syndrome," during the earliest days of his training as an organic chemist and physician. He noticed that many patients he was asked to see during his rounds all seemed to present similar nonspecific symptoms even though they had very different maladies. They all appeared to have high blood pressure, diminished appetite, weight loss, and looked exhausted. He later conducted experiments on rats, subjecting them to stressful situations furiously running on mazes and found that their bodies responded with adrenal hyperactivity, lymphatic atrophy, and bleeding peptic ulcers. He interpreted these changes to stressful situations as part of the syndrome he identified in which people attempt to accommodate demands but fall apart when they run out of gas.

Selye was an ambitious, driven workaholic who thought nothing of putting in 14-hour days in his laboratory, destroying his first two marriages and neglecting his five children along the way. Yet he claimed he absolutely loved his job, so much that he never described it as stressful or even work, but joyful.

There's an App or Oil for That

Nowadays we are besieged by articles, stories, talks, and advice telling us that stress is killing us because of the choices we make. We are urged to seek professional help, join self-help groups, medicate ourselves, all to deal with this overwhelming disease that has taken over our lives. There are even mobile apps that we can readily access on our phones, watches, or wristbands to constantly measure our stress levels and immediately practice mindful breathing or be reminded to slow down.

There are articles all over the internet with titles like "5 Instant Ways to Counteract Stress When You're Overwhelmed." One such piece recommends the standard simplistic solutions to a problem that is actually quite complex and multidimensional: Just take three deep breaths, or put on some music, or laugh it off, or do something kind. The featured photo with the article is a vial of cannabis oil, in case this advice doesn't quite do the job.

Since the implication of these devices and tools, as well as sage advice from stress experts, is that we should carefully monitor our stress levels, we become obsessed and hypervigilant in measuring responses to everything that occurs. Until Selye invented a word to describe this phenomenon, human beings believed that this was just a little uncomfortable but inevitable part of being alive. Of *course* you'd get overexcited if someone or something was threatening or challenging for you. Now we are informed this is a treatable medical condition that may require medication or interventions. We are told that stress is best studied by medical scientists in neuroimmunology, neurobiology, and neuropsychology because of its deleterious effects on our health.

However useful these studies about stress, it is hardly just a personal issue, but instead is affected by all kinds of things related to gender, sexual orientation, race, culture, age, profession, and experiences with such things as bullying, oppression, racism, marginalization, discrimination, and other injustices. Any strategy or program designed to respond to stress must take into consideration the person's previous subjective experience, perceptions, cognitive appraisal, life and work situation. Stress, like almost everything else we might examine, is best understood when we take into consideration physiological, psychological, environmental, and cultural factors. Likewise, any useful self-care plan that hopes to have enduring effects must also take these into consideration.

When Self-Care Is Just Another Burden

We are constantly being told that we don't take good enough care of ourselves, whether by the advertising or travel industries, the self-help industry, fitness clubs, luxury resorts, or the ethical codes of our professions. One psychiatrist admits to feeling in a bind. On one hand she feels exhausted and overwhelmed by the nature of her job and its demands on her time; on the other hand, the admonishment to take on more self-care feels like just another item on her to-do list. She wonders why this isn't working—for her or almost anyone else she knows. "It's because this faux self-care that we are being offered is not actually feeding us" (Lakshmin, 2018). Rather than adding something more to her plate, she feels that what would be far more advantageous is to set some limits and start enforcing clear boundaries. Specifically, for her situation, this means pausing every time someone asks her to do something and remembering she has several choices in how she could respond. She can agree to the added task, decline to do it, or more frequently, negotiate the requirements to something that feels reasonable and doable without adding to her stress.

Self-care has just become one more job that we are assigned, one more annoying responsibility, as if it is our own damn fault that we are floundering in the first place. Biologist Lewis Thomas (1975) remarked decades ago that the consensus among the medical establishment "is that we are badly designed, intrinsically fallible, vulnerable to a host of hostile influences inside and around us." They tell us that unless we are constantly and carefully checking our stress levels, and undertaking a sophisticated and consistent program of self-care, we are so fragile that we may very well implode.

That's all very considerate, to remind us to be careful when we subject our bodies and minds to excessive pressure, but this conception totally ignores the larger forces at work that are *way* beyond our control. This helps explain why the vast majority of people who count their steps, track their fitness and sleep, and wear watches and devices that measure their activities report that they feel increased guilt and pressure, as well as controlled by these devices that rule their lives. More than half see them as their nemesis or enemy.

The reality is that self-care is primarily a commercial commodity, marketed by businesses to sell products that are alleged to reduce daily stress and lead to enlightenment. There are thousands of apps to be downloaded on the phone, supposedly designed to hold us accountable, reminding us to breathe, meditate, stretch, or otherwise practice some form of mindfulness. There isn't much evidence to indicate that any of these technological marvels make much of a difference—except to add to the burdens of responsibility and subsequent guilt when we fail to stick with the regimen.

Subtracting Instead of Adding

Now that burnout is an officially recognized condition by the World Health Organization, even more enterprises have jumped on the bandwagon, offering supposedly simple, painless, convenient, accessible solutions to whatever ails us. The main problem, of course, is that today's work demands, regardless of the profession, keep us on duty 24 hours a day. If this sounds like an exaggeration, consider that something like 90% of young adults, 18 to 29 years old, sleep with their phones, and a significant number engage in "sleep texting" in which they receive a message in the middle of the night, wake up to reply to it, but then have no memory of doing so the next day. There is no longer any sanctuary in our lives once we are accessible every moment.

If the purpose of self-care is to improve the quality of our lives, as well as reduce excessive stress, then perhaps the goal is not so much to add one more thing to the burden as much as to reduce obligations and dismantle the system that is creating the problem (Havlin, 2019). Unfortunately, many self-care strategies are being sold based on the idea of increasing productivity and creating even further commitment to the job. One such plan promises "the secret to becoming a productivity powerhouse" that is designed to "ramp up your productivity—and squeeze more out of the time you are at work" (deBara, 2019).

Alas, a facial, massage, treadmill desk, or deep breathing exercise is not going to make much of a difference as long as we keep going at a furious pace, pressured to do more with less. It is time for us to look more critically at what is truly helpful and what often makes things so much worse. Unless we are prepared to invest the hard work in sustainable programs that really address the underlying issues of stress in our lives, we have no chance to make an indelible impact—either with our own lives or the lives of those we serve.

CHAPTER 2

Different Names, Similar Symptoms

The emotional states of worry and stress are relatively recent evolutionary phenomena in the human condition. During ancient times, the brain was smaller than its current configuration; there was little space and time to think too much about potential dangers in the future when people had enough to do just surviving the day. Humans lacked the capacity for sophisticated problem solving or even much systematic planning. They were concerned primarily with finding the next meal or escaping inclement weather.

Nowadays, however, we are constantly aware of every possible thing that could go wrong, anticipating during every spare moment all the possible disappointments, obstacles, threats, health concerns, and dangers that might befall us. Fluctuations in the stock market, interest rates, political elections, virus epidemics, expense reports, traffic conditions, and so many other things we can't control, lead to constant worry and a sense of helplessness. Perhaps it is no surprise that three quarters of adults report at least one major symptom of stress during the previous weeks and one third feel overwhelming, chronic stress in their jobs.

Once adaptations were required during the coronavirus pandemic, leading to further isolation, economic uncertainty, and fears, the stress levels were amplified significantly. "I used to think my job was incredibly difficult," one agency administrator said during a consultation, "but working from home has been so much more challenging, even without the commute to the office. Staff are often unavailable or don't follow through with things—and of course I understand why—but it just means that I am more overwhelmed than ever filling in the gaps."

All feelings, especially those related to stress and anxiety, are not some unique human capacity, as Harari (2018) points out, but rather they are biochemical reactions specifically designed to help us to quickly identify and anticipate dangers and react immediately to those potential *perceived* threats.

Obviously that perception is everything, since our survival depends on accurately reading those situations in which quick evasive action is required.

The concept of psychological stress is now thought to include any time that someone perceives a threat. Every system within the human body mounts a determined defensive response to the occupant's belief that some imagined danger is present. All perceptual systems continuously scan the physical and social environments for anything that could lead to injury, conflict, or even humiliation. This "fight or flight" reaction instantly calls upon internal resources to focus concentration, resist distractions, speed up reaction time, and access pure emotion, which leads to quick decisions that may be seem optimal at the time but ultimately have deleterious long-term consequences (Heid, 2019).

We've all been inundated with the effects of chronic, continuous overreactions that continue to flood cortisol, adrenaline, and hypervigilant thoughts through the body and mind. This creates a toxic condition that eventually leads to a variety of health threats, including elevated blood pressure, strokes, heart attacks, and desensitized immune functioning. In the case of health professionals, whose jobs require them to work with others suffering from various maladies, occupational hazards can develop that go under different names: burnout, compassion fatigue, vicarious trauma, secondary trauma, or existential crisis. Regardless of its particular form and diagnosis, the consequences are potentially devastating if left unchecked.

The Invention of Stress

As mentioned in the previous chapter, it was the great endocrinologist, Hans Selye, who carefully documented the idea of stress as a physiological and emotional phenomenon. He was also quite clear that it takes different forms depending on how people view their experiences. He was at first concerned primarily with *distress*, the coordinated bodily response to overwhelming and frightening circumstances, the sort that leads to hormonal and neurological overload and can become quite destructive and unhealthy over time. But he also observed that some other kinds of stress were relatively neutral (*neustress*) if they had no particular impact one way or the other. Eventually he came to define stress rather generally and neutrally as any nonspecific bodily response to some change that takes place in the environment. He viewed stress as a survival mechanism that evolved to heighten our senses and increase optimal performance in crucial situations.

Selye also observed that there were certain kinds of stress (*eustress*) that were experienced as relatively positive, even interesting and fun. These were situations in which the feelings were viewed as more challenging, intriguing, and stimulating than necessarily upsetting. That's the allure of riding roller coasters, taking constructive risks, signing up for adventures, taking on new responsibilities, trying new things, playing games, performing on stage, or speaking up in a meeting. This kind of stress often leads to growth, learning, and improved life satisfaction. It is considered an anecdote to boredom and complacency.

It's a myth that stress necessarily leads to depletion, discouragement, burnout, and similar disturbing emotional states. Rather, it's a particular *kind* of anxiety that is particularly detrimental. Acute stress can be quite exciting and stimulating; it's chronic stress that is the problem (see Table 2.1). In fact, it is the duration and intensity of the response that determines whether the results are experienced as essentially harmful or benign. As long as stress reactions don't continue for more than a few hours, their side effects can be successfully metabolized, and in many cases, actually enhance and strengthen the immune system (Dhabhar, 2019). That's one reason why physical exercise (which is really a form of controlled suffering) keeps the body and mind prepared and well-tuned to deal with adversities in life.

During the early 20th century, physiologist Walter Cannon made some of the first connections between internal disruptions of the body and external challenges. He was not only the first to call these physiological changes "stress," borrowing the term from the realm of physics, but also described the state of "homeostasis" that is thrown into disarray during such circumstances. During the decade following these discoveries, Hans Selye perilously warned the world about what he considered the most dangerous threat to humankind—when people are subjected to stressful conditions that make them "drunk with their own hormones." He was referring, of course, to the flood of cortisol, adrenaline, and norepinephrine that provide a surge of energy during perceived crisis situations.

Table 2.1 DISTINCTIONS BETWEEN DISTRESS AND EUSTRESS

Distress	Eustress
Experienced as frightening and disturbing	Experienced as exciting and stimulating
Perceived as an obstacle, annoyance, or inconvenience	Perceived as a challenge and opportunity
Pessimistic and discouraged mindset	Optimistic and hopeful mindset
Feelings of helplessness and passivity	Feelings of control and engagement
Limits effectiveness	Improves performance and productivity
Leads to anxiety, depression, and burnout	Leads to growth, learning, and resilience
Decreases life and work satisfaction	Increases sense of well-being and satisfaction

Burnout was first identified and described as a separate phenomenon almost 50 years later by Herbert Freudenberger (1974), a successful New York psychologist who was driven by ambition and a strong work ethic. He had been a survivor of the Holocaust, escaping to the United States when he was a young child. According to his daughter, "his childhood kind of stopped at 7 or 8 because he had then to grow up pretty quickly and survive in a new country" (King, 2016). As an orphan he was subjected to a number of indignities and abuse, wandering the streets as a homeless, lost child. He later dedicated his life to helping others among the dispossessed—especially addicts who lived on Skid Row. He ended up working two jobs, almost 18 hours a day, exhausted to the point he could barely get out of bed. He admitted that, at one point, he lost all joy and pleasure in his life, neglecting his family and suffering from a number of health problems that disrupted his sleep and appetite, not to mention his composure.

Eventually, Freudenberger came to terms with the extent his life was out of control, driven by the compulsive need to do more, to help more, to make up for the suffering he had experienced so early in life. He explained in an interview the origins of his thinking related to this phenomenon: "Burnout really is a response to stress. It's a response to frustration. It's a response to a demand that an individual may make upon himself in terms of a requirement for perfectionism or drive" (King, 2016).

Once he came to terms with what was happening to him, he identified a name for the condition, which he borrowed from a Graham Greene novel called *A Burnt-out Case* about a discouraged doctor working in Africa. Freudenberger realized he needed to structure time in his life for recovery and rejuvenation. He still refused to stop working so much because he was on a mission to make as much difference as he could in the lives of the haunted and afflicted, but he did start to set limits so he could spend more time with his family. At one point he proudly showed his daughter that he could just lie still on the surface of a lake in a "dead man's float," as a shining example of his commitment to take at least a few minutes each day to do absolutely nothing.

Freudenberger's initial description of his burned out condition was later expanded and popularized by Maslach (Maslach et al., 2001; Maslach, 2015) and others to consider a broader, more clearly defined context for the problem. The "burnout syndrome" is now considered by the World Health Organization to be a legitimate, formalized occupational stress disorder that is included in the International Classification of Diseases (World Health Organization, 2020). Although it refers more generally to any job responsibilities that lead to chronic, debilitating stress, the nature of being an emotional caregiver leads to a whole other set of challenges. It had also been discovered that professionals who work closely with people who have suffered severe trauma, neglect, or abuse are at greater risk of collateral damage and contagious effects. This became known as "secondary trauma," "vicarious trauma," and "compassionate fatigue," all of which can occur when professionals work within intimate helping relationships (Figley, 1983; Pearlman & Saakvitne, 1995). Whereas burnout refers generally to emotional and physical exhaustion, compassion fatigue relates more specifically to the inability to recover from the sustained pressures of emotional engagement in relationships. Vicarious trauma, on the other hand, is a potentially even more profound change in condition when we take on board the disturbing experiences and memories of traumatized clients. It isn't just that we are haunted by their stories, but that even hearing them can result in a major shift in our own worldview and essential beliefs.

Distinctions have been made between the various forms of stress reactions that afflict helping professionals, although perhaps the differences are not as clear as their various definitions might imply (see Table 2.2). Over time burnout has become synonymous with depression, since the symptoms are often quite similar. Although it was once used to refer to a mild case of work-related stress that led to dissatisfaction and unhappiness, it is now used far more globally to describe a general condition of poor functioning and low morale.

If you have ever worked with someone who has survived catastrophic, unimaginable suffering, it is difficult to *not* become affected by the encounter. Some of the narratives we've heard will plague us for the rest of our lives and irrevocably alter the way we see the world. I was asked to consult on a case in which a psychiatry resident was ordered by an attending surgeon to visit a patient who was still in the recovery room after all her toes and fingers had been amputated because of an untreated infection. The patient was a refugee, recently arrived in the country, who had been repeatedly refused medical treatment previously. The older, white male, a distinguished surgeon, was

Table 2.2 DISTINCTION BETWEEN VARIOUS PROFESSIONAL STRESS REACTIONS

Primary psychological trauma: a direct personal experience with some major crisis, incident, injury, or disaster that results in an inability to cope effectively; characterized by severe anxiety, depression, and perceived threat to security

Secondary trauma: stress reactions that result from close proximity to someone experiencing major trauma, especially as a result of a close, intimate relationship that was high in emotional valence

Vicarious trauma: contagious effects and emotional resonance as a result of listening, or being a witness, to a client's catastrophic trauma narrative

Compassion fatigue: acute and prolonged exposure to high levels of trauma and misfortune in a professional role, resulting in blurred boundaries, internalized negative feelings, and unconscious absorption of client's fears, anxieties, and hopelessness

Burnout: chronic stress on the job that results from interpersonal, administrative, workload, or political difficulties; results in reduced efficiency, physical and emotional exhaustion, cynicism, and loss of satisfaction

uncomfortable facing this patient after she regained consciousness, not wanting to be bothered to tell her what he did while she was under anesthesia. He called upon our unit to deal with this emotional stuff and the resident asked for my input as to what she should do.

For reasons I didn't understand at the time, I politely excused myself from the room for a few moments to regain my composure: I started crying. I just felt so helpless, so indignant, so furious. Most of my rage was directed at this arrogant doctor who believed that actually talking to patients wasn't within his province, but was "women's work," left to a psychiatry resident positioned at the bottom of the power hierarchy. I was triggered big time by this incident, reminded that the president had just ended all refugee resettlement and funding in our country. I felt so badly for the resident who was put in this situation and wanted me to tell her what to do. But most of all, I couldn't stop thinking (and still can't!) about this poor woman who was about to learn she lost most of her hands and feet before she would be put out on the street. Yes, my worldview changed, so much so that I decided to change the nature of my work in order to deal with accumulated vicarious trauma that had been growing within me during the previous year.

Burning or Rusting Out?

Burnout implies that the professional is going about their daily business, taking care of tasks, operating in a typical manner—and then WHAM!—he or she suddenly sputters out like an extinguished flame. This is hardly the case, since the process of erosion occurs over a longer period of time. It is a more gradual and insidious process that may more appropriately be called "rust-out," in the same manner that a substance slowly deteriorates and breaks down over time when subjected to noxious conditions.

We actually understand very little about the nature of burnout processes. Studies have found that anywhere from 20% to 60% of mental health professionals exhibit major symptoms, although it is estimated that about half experience this condition at some point in their careers (Jergensen, 2018). Perhaps not surprising, one's vulnerability is related to the chosen theoretical orientation: practitioners who employ mindfulness or cognitive-based skills appear to be somewhat better protected if they regularly practice their skills on themselves.

When helping professionals neglect themselves to the point where they not only lose joy in what they're doing but also sacrifice themselves in the process, burnout may often result. This is an insidious and progressive condition. Although some clinicians experience difficulties, as documented by the ways they count the minutes of their sessions and the days until retirement, many

Table 2.3 SYMPTOMS OF BURNOUT, COMPASSIONATE FATIGUE, AND STRESS DIFFICULTIES

- Emotional exhaustion
- Lack of physical energy
- Dispirited, pessimistic, negative attitudes
- Impaired concentration and focus
- Frequency of verbalized cynical, critical complaints
- Depersonalized view of clients as objects
- Feelings of ineptitude and disillusionment
- Feelings of anger or frustration at being victimized or marginalized
- Lack of meaning and satisfaction in work
- Feeling unsafe to express oneself honestly and authentically
- Feeling unsupported and unappreciated by colleagues
- Feelings of isolation and disengagement
- Collateral damage that affects family and friends
- Lack of personal coping and self-care strategies
- Sleep disruption due to intrusive thoughts
- Self-medication with drugs, alcohol, food, or behavioral addictions
- Physical complaints (headaches, stomachaches, digestive problems, etc.)
- Feelings of helplessness and futility to change situation and make impact

others show early signs without necessarily being aware of what is happening to them (see Table 2.3).

The manifestations of stress reactions can occur in a number of areas (Hydon et al., 2015), including physical (low energy, nausea, stomachaches, headaches, insomnia), behavioral (addictions, drug or alcohol abuse, self-defeating choices), cognitive (poor concentration, irrational thinking, poor decision making, hypervigilance, intrusive memories), emotional (numbness, depression, sadness, anxiety, powerlessness), interpersonal (detached, isolated, conflicted, mistrustful, impatient), spiritual (lack of meaning, loss of faith, questioning role and mission), and professional (diminished work performance, inefficiency, low morale).

There are certain conditions and particular hazards that are most likely to lead to, or exacerbate, stressful reactions among staff (see Table 2.4). These can relate to working conditions, organizational culture, client issues and behavior, or quite personal factors related to the professional's personality, attitudes, expectations, interpersonal style, and lifestyle, among others (Norcross & VandenBos, 2018).

After reviewing this extensive list, one can identify common themes related to a few influential factors. The first has to do with scheduling and time management, in which the demands of work exceed one's capacity to function at a consistently high level. The second major theme has to do with the climate and culture of the work environment, in which professionals are exposed to interpersonal conflict, lack of collegial support, poor or excessive administrative oversight, inefficiency, and supervisor neglect or incompetence.

Table 2.4 CONDITIONS THAT MOST CONTRIBUTE TO POOR MORALE AND BURNOUT

- Perceived lack of control over job responsibilities
- Confusing, unclear, or fluctuating expectations from administration
- Supervisor(s) perceived as incompetent or uncaring
- Supervision focused only on micromanaging procedures, policies, and tasks
- Minimal training opportunities
- Limited experience to complete assigned tasks
- Peer debriefing discouraged or unavailable
- Repetitive nature of work with little variability
- Chaotic, inefficient operation of organization
- Few opportunities for advancement or new responsibilities
- Conflict between personal and organizational values and priorities
- Toxic organizational culture with interpersonal conflicts
- Abuse of power by those in control
- Time pressures and excessive work hours
- Norms that allow for backstabbing or undermining others
- Competitive atmosphere that leads to power inequities
- Perceived low compensation and minimal benefits
- Presence of a bully or abusive, insensitive staff member
- Incidences of racism, discrimination, microaggressions, or marginalization
- Unfair and inequitable rewards for productivity
- Lack of resources and appropriate funding
- High staff turnover
- Unreasonable workload and caseload
- Excessive paperwork, monitoring, and documentation
- Disinterest by administration to address staff morale
- Severely distressed, traumatized, chronic clients
- Personal disruptions (loss, health issues, transitions, finances)

Different Flavors

So far we've been looking at burnout, rust-out, or work stress as if it is a singular entity that strikes professionals in the same way. Similar to depression, anxiety, or any other emotional difficulty, there are several different types that manifest themselves in unique ways (Farber & Heifetz, 1982; Montero-Marin et al., 2014). It has always been interesting, if not fascinating, observing the ways our clients—and colleagues—appear to react so differently to adversity and life challenges.

Here are a few different ways that stress reactions are experienced.

Overload burnout: This professional just works too hard, too long, too much, without sufficient satisfaction, leading to physical and emotional exhaustion. One's significant goals and aspirations feel stifled.

Wearout (or rust-out): This is due primarily to feelings of discouragement and disappointments that have occurred over time. Frustration and helplessness result. The person goes through the motions of doing the absolute minimum to just get through the day.

Underchallenged burnout: Boredom and tedium set in because of the perceived repetitive nature of the job. Many clients start to sound the same. There are few opportunities for growth or new challenges. The person feels unappreciated and undervalued, leading to cynicism and disengagement.

Neglect: There is a marked loss of passion, commitment, and motivation because of a sense of helplessness to change things. This results in complacency and acceptance of mediocrity.

Soulful sufferers: This professional adopts a martyr complex due to feeling inadequate and unappreciated to an extreme degree. He or she develops more severe, chronic symptoms that lead to depression and anxiety.

Stretched superstars: They develop unrealistic expectations and unbridled ambition that lead them to try to do far too much, given what is realistic and possible.

None of these types must necessarily lead to a degree of serious impairment, even if they do reduce optimal functioning and effectiveness.

You can test yourself to determine your own vulnerability at this particular moment by rating each of the following items on a scale of 1 to 3, with 1 indicating that the symptom is not present, 3 indicating that it is definitely present, and 2 meaning that you're not sure.

- I catastrophize or exaggerate consequences.
- I find it difficult to stay present in sessions. My mind wanders. I am prone to fantasy. My attention is constantly diverted.
- I feel increasing impatience toward my clients, colleagues, or both.
- I feel cynical, suspicious, and judgmental toward many clients.
- I feel a lack of support, or even active conflict or disagreement, with many colleagues.
- I feel resistant to going to work in the morning.
- I feel minimally invested in the quality of my work.
- I feel more than a little relieved when clients cancel appointments.
- Work feels routine, predictable, boring, and without challenge.
- I notice stress symptoms that are interfering with my sleep and other daily functioning.
- I feel isolated and alienated.
- I fantasize a lot about doing something else.

Add up your score, divide it by the number of years you've been practicing, multiply by your shoe size ... just kidding! The total score doesn't mean much. What's important is that you've just completed an honest assessment of the extent to which you are experiencing any of these feelings. The operative word in the previous sentence is "extent," because burnout is not only gradual, but falls on a continuum. Almost all of us feel burned out at times. It is a problem when it becomes chronic, leads to destructive behavior, interferes with the quality of our lives and the effectiveness of our work, and is not addressed by ongoing self-care strategies.

The Problems With Self-Care

As discussed previously, self-care is often marketed and sold as the be-all and end-all, the royal road to living happily ever after. Alas, more often than not such efforts result in disappointment, frustration, and increased demoralization. Self-care is not just some singular attempt to include a new habit that fixes all that is unbalanced. We've reviewed how stress itself is hardly a global term, but rather refers to so many different kinds of reactions, depending on whether it is acute or chronic, intermittent or continuous, or perceived as harmful, interesting, or fun. That is one reason it has been suggested that the word itself is so confusing and ill-defined (Francis, 2018).

Self-care is usually described as some activity that is specifically designed to facilitate, promote, ensure, or restore high psychological functioning and health, especially in response to direct (or vicarious) trauma or life disruption. It is most effectively implemented *before* a tipping point in which the levels of stress become too overwhelming (Mavridis et al., 2019).

Just as there are different names and terms for experiences of stress and discouragement, so too are there distinctions between what comprises self-care versus attempts at self-soothing behavior. People do all kinds of things to provide comfort to themselves when under pressure (or bored). They sing, dance, listen to music, masturbate, take a bubble bath, smoke weed or drink wine, go shopping, play games, or attend a retreat. Likewise, articles appear in the media promoting "genius products to eliminate stress," suggesting ridiculously that purchasing a fidget toy, herbal tea, weighted blanket, oil diffuser, or a cooling face mask will cure whatever is wrong. Yet these actions usually just offer a temporary respite from difficulties, hardly qualifying as any kind of meaningful, long-lasting solution. A clear demarcation must thus be made between efforts that are merely self-indulgent and those that lead to self-compassion and much deeper understanding of the forces at work that obscure meaningful engagement. The point is made that true self-care is not just reactive to something going on, but rather creates enduring, supportive foundations for everything else we do (Neo, 2020).

In order for self-care efforts to have lasting, significant impact, reducing negative stressors and increasing resilience and hardiness to immunize us against challenges at work and in daily life, it is important to understand what must be included, as well as what simply wastes time and energy.

Requires Acknowledgment of Difficulties

Given our training and expertise, we have at our disposal dozens of effective ways to deny, minimize, or otherwise avoid some of the realities that plague us. Yes, we are highly skilled at diagnosing others' problems, but also well prepared to make excuses for why our own issues are not really that serious. Just as we are sometimes not very accurate in our assessment of how well things are working in our helping relationships, we are inclined to shrug off annoying and unpleasant symptoms. Just like our clients, we engage in wishful thinking that things will improve of their own accord if just given enough time.

Promises Instant Relief

Get a massage. Drink a green smoothie. Go for a walk. Schedule a manicure. There has been an overemphasis on specific techniques and strategies, not to mention self-care products, that are alleged to make all the difference. And of course they don't—for very long—especially when we return to the same conditions and forces that continue outside of our control. Just as in every other aspect of life, it's rare that any quick-fix tool or technique will make much of a significant difference, at least one that has enduring impact. With respect to self-care, the evidence is also pretty compelling that broad, personally designed and contextualized strategies are far more likely to work (Colman et al., 2016; Norcross & VandenBos, 2018).

Implies Something Is Broken

Let's face it: something probably *is* broken in the sense that the current situation isn't working. We are supposed to be experts, high-functioning muses who represent the ideal of mental health. Understandably, we may be reluctant to admit to others, much less ourselves, that things feel out of control. Who wants to feel like a hypocrite that we aren't practicing in our own lives what we tell others to do?

Changes Don't Last

If the average number of times that someone makes the same exact New Year's resolution is 10, it is pretty evident that all of us have trouble sticking to our promises. Even vacations and holiday trips, designed as self-care interventions, don't have much enduring effect, considering that almost half of those returning from a vacation say that that the reduction of stress and restoration of energy lasts less than two days (American Psychological Association, 2018).

Deeper Issues

There are often underlying issues at work that lead to, or exacerbate, stress reactions. Self-care strategies may get at the most obvious, annoying symptoms but do not address the chronic, entrenched patterns that are operating to make things so much more difficult. These could be unacknowledged problems from the past (trauma, abuse, neglect), chronic health difficulties, family problems, interpersonal conflicts, personality features, addictions or substance abuse, or more nebulous existential questions in which there is loss of personal meaning in work and life.

Limits of Self-Help

There's only so much we can do for ourselves without assistance, support, and guidance from others, especially professionals. We might not have any compunction in taking our car for service, or calling a plumber when the toilet needs repair, but there is reluctance and resistance at times to get the help we need when we can't do it ourselves.

Reconceptualizing Self-Care

When discussing the subject of "self-care," it's important to acknowledge the changing perceptions of the very nature of the "self." Traditionally and historically, work stress was viewed as an imbalance or tension between personal and professional roles. Thus it was suggested that the essential self be protected and isolated from professional job responsibilities that were seen as eroding our spirit. The personal and professional selves were considered different entities altogether, separated from one another by clear boundaries. And yet, more recently, the two roles have come to be viewed as far more integrated—who we are at work and at home are just different aspects of the self, each of which affects, informs, and influences the other—for better or worse (Bressi & Vaden, 2017). It is a reality of our daily existence that experiences from each domain bleed into the other. Rather than this only being a possible source of stress, it is actually one of the incredible gifts of being a healer and helper: what we learn in our daily lives helps us to better understand and assist our clients, just as their stories and struggles provide us with insights and deeper understanding of our own issues.

The traditional and most popular view of self-care is that it becomes necessary when our professional roles and responsibilities "pollute" and "infect" our personal lives to the extent that stress symptoms become intolerable. Likewise, such evidence of burnout or compassionate fatigue occur in the opposite scenario, when aspects of our personal lives affect our ability to remain objective, compassionate, and optimally effective in our work. We have all kinds of names for this phenomena in the literature—countertransference, projective identification, biases—all of which imply a loss of objectivity and professionalism. The primary goal of self-care efforts has thus been designed to better demarcate the personal and professional selves, as if they are distinctly different entities. This is all the more peculiar when we consider that helping professionals rarely talk about their work in terms of, "I *do* psychotherapy," or "I *practice* nursing," or "I *teach*." Rather than using verbs, we define our core identities in terms of who we really are, or at least a significant part of who we are: I *am* a doctor or a nurse or a social worker or a teacher or a counselor or a supervisor.

We hardly switch off our training, knowledge, and deep understanding of the human condition when not on the clock. We don't improve our effectiveness only through sanctioned continuing education programs. Everything we have learned, and continue to learn every single day, (theoretically) increases our own personal and professional effectiveness in a variety of ways: our clients are actually our greatest teachers (Kottler & Carlson, 2006; Kottler, 2018). It is one of the greatest gifts and benefits of our work that we are offered so many opportunities to learn and grow from our conversations with others—in every setting and situation.

The idea that self-care ought to be focused on better separating the personal and professional selves is quite at odds with the realities of the ways we function in the world. The different parts of ourselves are not in competition with one another; they are not necessarily feuding for attention and dominance even if it sometimes feels that way with perceived limited time. More contemporary post-modern, constructivist, or relational models suggest that each of us has a multitude of selves, which are individually and uniquely negotiated in every relationship with a person, activity, or situation (DeYoung, 2015). This is all the more compelling when we consider that the primary tool of most helping professionals, regardless of specialty, is the *use of the self*. It is through the filters of our own experience (and training) that we collect data, identify difficulties, formulate diagnoses or label problems, and prescribe or suggest solutions.

In addition, the self does not exist in isolation, but is very much embedded in the norms, practices, rituals, and demands of the larger cultures with which we affiliate. There are so many social, political, environmental, organizational, and cultural pressures that also impinge on the options available to us. The stress and burnout that we may experience hardly result solely from our own unresolved or pressing personal issues, but are very much a part of the larger systems of which we are members. Even the current proliferation of resources devoted to stress, estimated to be 10 times more prevalent than just a decade ago, are as responsible for the obsession with the subject as anything else (Becker, 2013).

One corporate warrior (Marsh, 2011), whose life felt out of control because of his incessant work schedule that didn't allow him to spend more than minimal time with his partner and four children, realized that it wasn't until he was fired from his job that he could really consider looking at what others absurdly call "life-work balance." It is the imperatives from our culture that impose insane working hours and commitment that don't permit time to do the things we say are most important. He points out that the ways organizations are structured to maximize productivity don't really allow for the ideal to which we all strive. "And the reality of the society that we're in," he explains, "is there are thousands and thousands of people out there leading lives of quiet, screaming desperation, where they work long, hard hours at jobs they hate, to enable them to buy things they don't need, to impress people they don't like."

When we consider the job pressures, work responsibilities, and emotional arousal that are associated with any helping profession, plus the nature of the organizations that rule our lives, as well as their priorities, policies, and administrative oversight, it is clear that there is only so much relief that will occur by joining a gym or working from home a few days each week. If anything, the workweek has now been expanded to 120 hours, as long as we are tethered to our mobile devices. Half of all American workers never even bother to use all their entitled vacation days!

Self-care is, therefore, not just about taking a yoga class, scheduling a vacation, or working fewer hours; it is a process of self-discovery, meaning-making, and exploration of core values as they are expressed in daily lives (Bressi & Vaden, 2017). A certain amount of emotional distress associated with our work is not only to be expected but an absolutely normal part of our jobs. How can we not feel concerned, apprehensive, bothered, conflicted, and disturbed by some of the stories we hear? How can we not become profoundly moved by the suffering people we seek to help? How can we not be continually frustrated and stymied by the limits of what we can do—especially with those who are facing such intractable, horrifying experiences?

CHAPTER 3

Nature of the Work With No Place to Hide

During the 1920s, traffic in Manhattan was so awful that over a thousand people died each year of accidents, four times the number today. Between the muddy roads, streetcars, horses, and thousands of primitive vehicles, whomever attempted to navigate via automobile would usually find themselves at a complete standstill. Walking was often a far better alternative.

In an effort to reduce the fatalities and congestion, New York first attempted to install traffic lights, with no discernable effect. Eventually they decided to undertake the most ambitious, challenging engineering project since the construction of the Egyptian pyramids: they would build the longest underwater tunnel in the world, spanning over a mile and a half beneath the river. This would require seemingly insurmountable difficulties with the boring and excavation operation and ventilation system that took almost a decade just in the planning stages. It was expected that the risks associated with driving the "highway under the Hudson" would likely poison any driver foolish enough to undertake such a journey. And if the car fumes didn't kill you, then leaks from rushing water would surely lead to catastrophic drowning.

John Holland was hired as the chief engineer of this massive, daunting project. He had already demonstrated some expertise in tunnel construction by building subways underneath the city, but this mammoth task seemed almost impossible because of the insurmountable difficulties related to preventing people from expiring from water pressure or noxious fumes. He performed over 2,000 experiments from which to invent new technologies and construct 84 gigantic fans to clean the air. He was laboring away at a furious pace and all the while being pressured by politicians, donors, city administrators, and the public to get the job done.

Alas, before this engineering marvel could be completed, John Holland had a nervous breakdown from all the stress and was sent to a mental hospital to recover. He died of a heart attack from the stress of his job at the age of 43.

There is some interesting irony to this story. First of all, it was clear that it wasn't Holland's weakness of spirit or health that killed him as much as the stress from this difficult work, since his successor, Milton Friedman, also died of a heart attack soon after taking over the project. Secondly, as anyone in New York will attest, driving through the Holland Tunnel is now among the most stressful experiences on the planet for the 40 million drivers who brave the commute each year.

This is just one example of how the demands of a particular job can place incalculable pressure on people who try so hard for a degree of excellence, especially when others' health, safety, and well-being are at stake. Besides soldiers in combat, air traffic controllers, and police officers, helping professionals are among the most challenged. Physicians have the highest rate of suicide of any other profession, and the specialty most at risk of all is psychiatry. Eight out of ten practicing psychotherapists report serious episodes of depression or anxiety in the previous few years, plus major relationship conflicts. There is something about professions that demand so much commitment, responsibility, and excellence that place inordinate pressure on those who must operate under these conditions.

Health professionals and healers throughout the ages have known the risks and accepted the inevitable self-sacrifices that are part of the job. One of my very first books over 40 years ago was launched after an indigenous healer, a *curandero* in the Amazon, warned me that I must protect myself from the contagious effects of the people I help because it is likely that I would become infected by their suffering, which was believed to be the result of evil spirits. Even though his explanation was at odds with scientific evidence, he was not far wrong in his conclusions.

Throughout the history of medicine, especially infectious diseases, some of the most notable figures paid the ultimate price for their efforts to advance knowledge and continue their investigations into the causes of catastrophic conditions that have almost wiped out the human population at various times. In reviewing a "who's who" of such heroic individuals, Bryson (2019) mentions several of the most tragic stories. Theodor Bilharz, considered the father of tropical medicine, experimented with attaching parasitic worms to his stomach in order to follow the pathway of their burrowing into his liver. Howard Ricketts, a 19th century bacteriologist, perished while attempting to stop a typhus epidemic. Jesse Lazear, who was studying yellow fever during the beginning of the 20th century, died after deliberately infecting himself with the disease. Marie Curie, the only scientist to ever win Nobel Prizes in two different fields (chemistry and physics), enjoyed notoriety but two of her lab assistants died of radiation poisoning. More recently, during the coronavirus pandemic, Mei Zhongming, the doctor who tried to warn the world about a dangerous new disease, expired soon after his discovery.

We may not be in mortal danger from the clients we treat but we certainly catch their fears and are haunted by their tragic stories. With eyes and ears and heart wide open, we willingly enter into the arena with people who are bleeding despair and hopelessness. How could we ever hope to escape unscathed?

Additional Risks for Those Who Live to Serve

Given that stress, job dissatisfaction, and burnout have become somewhat universal problems across the spectrum of careers, what is it about being a helping professional that creates such additional risks that it leads almost half of us to become immobilized by pressures, stress, and burnout at some point in our careers?

The most obvious reason, of course, is that we live to serve. Almost by definition, our very existence is based on the assumption that personal sacrifices are the essence of the job in all kinds of ways. We resist meeting our own needs. We engage in relationships that are one-sided and designed exclusively to suspend our own best interests. In the same way that firefighters and law enforcement personnel risk their lives, we risk our emotional health and safety. Medical staff literally risk infections and catching their patients' diseases; we are prone to the contagious effects of others' despair and hopelessness. We listen to, and hold, the most pitiful, tragic stories imaginable and are charged with the responsibility for helping people recover from those experiences. It is no wonder that emotional exhaustion and depletion are the most common symptoms of burnout reported by so many practitioners, mostly the result of excessive workload and time pressures (McCormack et al., 2018).

We may often feel caught between two powerful forces. First is the pressure to agree to more and more commitments and responsibilities, leading to emotional and physical exhaustion. Alternatively, if we try to set limits, this may lead to feelings of guilt and inadequacy. Because our most singular professional strength is the ability and willingness to take the perspective of others, to see things from their point of view, we struggle constantly with regulating the boundaries between the needs of others and ourselves (Skovholt & Trotter-Mathison, 2016). This is particularly the case with beginners in the field, who have yet to learn ways to moderate workload, roll with the inevitable disappointments and setbacks, and set expectations that are realistic and attainable. Beginning therapists have yet to learn how to deal with all the confusion, ambiguity, and complexity that are part of the job. They are still trying to figure out if they have the "right stuff" to succeed in this profession over the long haul, an uncertain prospect given all the things for which they feel unprepared. What they may lack in experience, however, beginners can compensate with their unbridled enthusiasm and passion.

It is a reassuring message for beginners that what they may lack in experience, preparation, and training is made up for, in part, by the incredible excitement, passion, and enthusiasm attached to this new, amazing profession. On some level it is almost hard to believe how fortunate one feels to have been permitted to join our remarkable profession, to be trusted with this sacred mission of serving others. Yes, it can be draining and frustrating at times. Yes, we are usually underpaid and overworked. Yes, our clients can be challenging and our colleagues less than supportive. Yes, it is a pain to deal with licensing, continuing education, and all the bureaucratic, administrative tasks. Yes, we can easily become triggered by the issues brought into session. And yet with all these risks and responsibilities there is still no comparable job in which we are privileged to accompany people on their most important life journeys.

Feel It in Your Bones

Think of a client you have seen (or someone you helped), now or in the past, who has impacted you in some significant way, for better or worse. This is a person with whom you enjoyed a moving, intimate, profoundly meaningful encounter, perhaps leading to significant progress and transformation. Or perhaps it was someone who triggered tremendous frustration, confusion, uncertainty, helplessness, or perhaps fear and trepidation.

Bring this individual vividly to mind. Recall his or her manner, voice, style, and characteristic behavior. Replay a conversation that seemed particularly representative of your interactions with one another, one that feels powerfully memorable.

Now, notice the feelings that well up inside you, the sensations in your body. Which thoughts bubble to the surface? What reactions stick with you?

As we are certainly well aware, emotional responses are as contagious as viruses. They can infect us just as potently as any flu, especially when our empathic resonance is operating at the highest capacity. We are deliberately trying to *feel* what our clients are experiencing, to know (or approximate) their internal processing. Then there are the unconscious reactions that are being involuntarily sparked, those beyond our awareness. There's little doubt that we are often vulnerable to emotional contagion, taking on others' negative feelings in much the same way we might catch a cold. This tendency is significantly heightened in relationships in which empathy plays a strong part, coupled with the ways we attempt to synchronize our nervous systems so as to better read and make sense of client disclosures (Flora, 2019; Hatfield et al., 2014). In other words, hanging out all day with people who are bleeding emotionally and leaking suffering necessarily takes some toll on our own psyches—no matter how vigilant and prepared we might be.

Not surprisingly, experience not only can erode passion and enthusiasm over time but can also help immunize therapists against burnout and emotional exhaustion (Rupert & Dorociak, 2019). With aging, practitioners tend to develop inner resources to take stressors and challenges in stride, as well as to better maintain their self-care strategies. That is one reason why beginning practitioners are far more likely to feel dissatisfied with their jobs and be more inclined to quit when things get tough and they feel overwhelmed (Dorociak et al., 2017).

Some Reasons Why the Job Is So Stressful and Demanding

While there is little doubt why being a helping professional is such a satisfying and fulfilling career, there are also some very good reasons why there is a price paid for this choice.

Putting Others First

It is a foundation of helping and healing that we must exhibit extraordinary self-discipline, self-control, and self-restraint at all times. We are not permitted to meet our own needs. We are cautioned to maintain careful boundaries that are never to be crossed. No matter how provocative, challenging, even abusive a client might be, we must keep our cool and take things in stride. We are not allowed to lose our temper, to lash out, or otherwise engage in actions that might further antagonize those within our care. No matter how well prepared we might be to maintain equanimity in the face of tests and conflicts, there are inevitable lapses of patience and control.

Isolation and Compartmentalization

One of the biggest contributors to workplace stress in any profession is related to feelings of isolation and loneliness, affecting 60% of employees. In one survey it was found that close to half of workers say they have few, if any, meaningful relationships on their jobs as a result of a culture that discourages such interactions and provides little, if any, social support (Renken, 2020). People say they don't feel understood by their coworkers and become exhausted trying to engage with others in social activities. True intimacy with anyone is reported as rare because everyone seems so busy with their own priorities.

For therapists, the isolation is even more of a challenge. It is the nature of our work that we are completely insulated in carefully soundproofed rooms to ensure perfect privacy and confidentiality. Except for the brief intervals between sessions, we spend most of our time alone with our clients, rarely afforded many opportunities during the day to debrief or just have a conversation with some-one who doesn't want anything from us. We are prohibited from even talking about our sessions, and the disturbing things we heard, except to a designated supervisor, who is not usually available when we need to vent the most.

Intimate and Intense Nature of the Encounters

People disclose all kinds of things to us that they've never shared with anyone else before. They trust us in ways they never imagined were possible. They can't help but feel great affection, respect, and caring for someone who is so willing to listen carefully and respond so compassionately. It is also no surprise that we would have strong feelings toward those with whom we have spent such intimate conversations. Since the interactions are so spirited and intense, so filled with meaningful and significant discussions, it would be impossible not to be affected by them. Long after clients have left our offices, we are still left with swirling thoughts and confusing feelings inside our heads, trying to make sense of what happened and why.

Personal Triggers and Processes

This isn't just about countertransference reactions but *all* the internal dialogue that takes place while we are conducting sessions. Clients bring up issues all the time that resonate with our own experience or highlight some issue we have yet to fully resolve. So much of the time we are speaking to clients we are also talking to ourselves. They bring up conflicts that remind us of our own. They resemble people from our past with whom we have left things unsaid. They question and challenge some of our most cherished beliefs that require us to rethink where we stand. At times they deliberately do and say things just to get underneath our skin or keep us off balance. Most of all, they elicit our own sense of helplessness when we can't seem to get through to them in the way we'd prefer.

Resistances Within and Without

In spite of what our clients tell us, most of the time they have a certain ambiv-alence about what we are offering to them. They want definitive answers. They want instant results, preferably with minimal effort and absolutely no discomfort. Although they tell us they are willing to cooperate, to do anything required, that is rarely the case. We not only expect a certain degree of resistance, obstruction, and deception from clients, but become suspicious if someone appears to be a little too enthusiastic about how much fun they are having in sessions.

Then there is the reality that anything we try to do is often undermined or sabotaged by others who feel threatened by the changes taking place. We can complete the most powerful, enlightening session imaginable, send the client on their way with unbridled excitement, and then find that nothing has changed when the person returns the following week. There are just too many temptations, toxic influences, dysfunctional relationships, and impediments in the person's life to keep any momentum going.

Boredom and Repetition

The challenge of having too much stimulation, emotional arousal, and drama in our sessions is often counteracted by a few clients we see that insist on boring us, and everyone else in their lives, to distraction. They repeat themselves over and over, wallowing in self-pity. They tell the same stories repeatedly, even when we try to interrupt or redirect them. For those of us who have been practicing for many years, there is also the reality that many of our clients start to sound the same. We hear the beginning tale of a new referral and can't help but think to ourselves, "Okay, another one of *those* again," as if we are about to relive a conversation we've repeated many times before (which perhaps is true. In any case it is sometimes difficult to remain energized and focused when it feels like we are functioning on autopilot. This complacency, and failure to see each client as a unique and special, provides early indications it is time to change things up in some significant way.

Managed Care and Loss of Autonomy

The number one thing that all health professionals complain about is the amount of charting, paper work, administrative chores, and accountability that is required on the job. No matter what we think might be best for our clients, we are still required to secure approval from administrators, supervisors, team members, review boards, and insurance companies. They may decide to handicap our efforts in countless ways, limiting the number of sessions, mandating the type of treatment we are to deliver, demanding justification for every clinical decision and evidence that every intervention led to an empirically supported measurable outcome. This is not only annoying but exhausting and demoralizing.

Lack of Consensus and Agreement

If only there was one definitive, appropriate approach to treat a client complaint. It is one of the most frustrating, confusing aspects of our profession that someone could consult a half dozen different therapists and receive just as many different diagnoses and treatment plans. In spite of the overwhelming evidence that only a few factors make the most difference in positive outcomes, none of which relate to theoretical orientation or chosen techniques and instead are connected to the client's feelings of being heard and understood, we still spend an inordinate amount of time arguing with one another about whose theoretical framework is best and which of the latest innovations make everything else we know and understand obsolete. Even though we know that therapists don't even practice in sessions what they say they do, and that there is such a disconnect between what we think matters the most versus what clients tell us helped them the most, we still insist that whatever model we favor is far superior to all the rest. This lack of agreement contributes to added stress and uncertainty because whatever it is that we do there will be a crowd of other colleagues who tell us we are doing it wrong.

Political Realities

Speaking of colleagues and coworkers, in many agencies and organizations staff don't function very well together. There is a competitive atmosphere, perceptions of inequity, feelings of neglect or disrespect, a lack of structure—or too much oversight. It is difficult to navigate the complex interpersonal conflicts that have been festering over time, often the result of alliances that only wish to maintain power. Whereas private practitioners often complain the most about isolation and loneliness, agency staff report the opposite difficulty of feeling exhausted by the interpersonal drama on a daily basis. Scheduled and impromptu staff meetings can feel like a snake pit in which coalitions compete with one another for attention, priorities, and resources. If administrative support and supervision are less than ideal, conflicts and competition can easily spin out of control.

Martyr Mentality

Let's be honest: sometimes we really do feel special. We know and understand things that escape most others. What we do for a living is help solve problems that appear hopeless. We are good talkers, able to explain ideas in ways that make them more accessible. We also demonstrate incredible composure, patience, and indulgence during times of crisis. Yes, we are special. At times we feel invincible, so much so that we forget we are flawed, needy human beings. We take our deprivations and suffering in stride, believing it just comes with the territory. Yet it is precisely that belief that prevents us from taking the preventive steps to take better care of ourselves.

Confusion, Complexity, and Ambiguity

The nature of psychological aid is that we can never be really certain if, or when, we actually helped anyone. Clients lie. A lot. Those who tell us we were miracle workers who made all the difference are directly contradicted by what we witness or what we are told by others. That's certainly bewildering, but not as frustrating as those who deny any progress and attack us for incompetence while it is absolutely clear to us and others that they have been completely transformed. How can we ever really know for sure when we have "fixed" anyone?

Sense of Helplessness and Futility

Let's face it: Change takes time, especially meaningful, lasting transformations that make a real difference. The pacing of therapy is often glacial, intermittent, spotty, and marked by relapses and failures. Unlike our medical colleagues, who have all kinds of fancy scanning and biomedical devices to determine what is going on, therapists rely on listening and talking. It almost sounds ridiculous that this is considered a viable, legitimate procedure.

There are so many people who come to us with chronic, intractable problems, many of which will never fully go away no matter what we—or anyone else—might do. The nature of the systemic dysfunction within the family, the organic basis of the symptoms, the level and degree of impairment, all considerably impact the ultimate prognosis and the extent of recovery that may be possible.

Personal Triggers

Motives for becoming a helper and healer in the first place are not just altruistic; they are also self-serving. Most of us gravitated to this profession not just to save the world, but also to save ourselves in some way. Perhaps some of us are working toward redemption for our own mistakes and miscalculations, or working through feelings of helplessness and powerlessness, or a sense of impotence, or other unresolved issues of the past that relate to our family of origin. In any case, becoming a therapist is the perfect throne from which to increase one's sense power and control: all day long pilgrims travel great distances, at great expense and inconvenience, just to hear our words of wisdom and feel our healing spirit.

Being a therapist provides not just the opportunity to believe, but the illusion, that we are omnipotent beings with the capacity to fix things in others' lives, things that we may not have been able to deal with in our own. We are afforded a window into people's most private, secret lives, feeding a voyeuristic desire for the forbidden. We are able to live vicariously through the misdeeds and triumphs of those we help. We can rescue people in the throes of impending crisis and thereby satisfy a need for meaningful significance—to feel that we truly matter in some way. We can work through our own problems and difficulties, all the while convincing others to do the things we wish to do. We get to feel like a know-it-all, someone who has gotten things together.

If these are some of the personal incentives for becoming a helper and healer, then there are some features of certain clients, or particular therapeutic relationships, or contextual factors within the treatment, that definitely lead to significantly increased stress and emotional arousal, and even trigger unresolved issues. This begins with a mismatch between expectations and actual realistic possibilities. In some cases, our own hopes are wildly inaccurate or improbable: We actually believe we have the power to cure suffering with a wave of a magic wand or incantations—and then feel discouraged and frustrated when things don't proceed according to plan. More often, our clients have expectations for immediate, long-lasting relief, and then blame us for the seemingly glacial pace of progress.

In other cases, we become triggered by feelings of incompetence or failure because of a mismatch between certain clients and what we can reasonably offer. Sometimes it is a matter of personality clashes, limitations of our treatment approach, or some breach in the alliance that was sparked by some remark or action we can't even identify. Other times such impasses may result from impatience on our part, because a client is just not ready yet to move forward with the determination we would prefer. In other cases, the presenting problems are conceptualized in a way that makes them virtually impossible to fix, and clients are resistant to reframing them in a more amenable way; they blame bad luck, genetic predispositions, fate, the economy, or believe that everything is everyone else's fault.

Almost by definition, many clients are seeing us in the first place because they are too difficult and challenging for others to handle. They say and do all kinds of annoying things designed to push others away; in a sense, that is their essential job in life, since they appear to thrive on others' discomfort with their behavior. Needless to say, it is inevitable when working with severely depressed, anxious, or otherwise disturbed individuals that the going is going to be tough at times, that we will be abused, confused, and stymied no matter how hard we work.

Then there is all the deception that takes place among our clients, how they pretend to be someone or something they are not, how they make up all kinds of stories that are clearly not true, how they hide or disguise aspects of themselves that are crucial to understanding what is really going on. As mentioned, clients sometimes lie boldly to us, and to themselves. They may deceive us in a multitude of ways, often beyond their awareness but sometimes just to mess with us, to inflate their own sense of power by trying to knock us off our pedestals. All of this may reflect their own ambivalence and uncertainty regarding really wanting to change in the first place. On some level they may be enjoying the toxic power they wield over others.

We are expected to suffer silently the slings and arrows directed our way, the outbursts of indignation, the testing of limits. We are constrained by various rules, regulations, bureaucratic policies, limited resources, and ethical imperatives that require us to remain dispassionate, controlled, and calm in the face of emotional storms. This can trigger us in other ways as we hold inside ongoing frustrations. The single most common symptom of burnout and toxic occupational stress is emotional exhaustion. It is no wonder that we become worn down by the requirement of constant empathic resonance and compassionate caring in the face of interpersonal onslaughts.

If all this doesn't push our buttons and keep us off balance at times, then we surely become aroused by how difficult it is to assess how well we are actually doing. Remember, clients are not usually completely honest and disclosing. They tell us things are going well when, in fact, things are slowly falling apart. They complain therapy isn't helping at all when significant others in their lives report startling changes. Some clients just disappear and we never learn what happened to them. Other cases that we imagined were spectacular successes turn out to be miserable failures after all. We can never be sure who we really helped and who we failed.

It is so difficult to measure success when there are so many different ways to assess progress. We can't even determine, with much reliability, who among us is most exceptional as practitioners (Kottler, 2017; Kottler & Carlson, 2015). Does it relate most to having a full case load, reputation in the community, recognition by colleagues, supervisor evaluations, reports by clients, fame and notoriety, or perhaps just self-promotion and effective marketing? One thing is for sure, we certainly can't rely on practitioner self-evaluations, considering that 80% of therapists believe themselves to be far better than their peers in their clinical outcomes **(Sapyta, Reiimer, & Bickman, 2005)**.

We tell our clients it is senseless, if not a complete waste of time, to whine and complain about things that are outside of one's control or just an inevitable part of life. And yet it is clear that what comes with the territory of being a healer is that we must deal with some very difficult people during times of their lives when they are at their worst. It is also almost a certainty that we will feel at times to be unappreciated, undercompensated, neglected, and abused. And the nature of the work means that we operate so often in an isolated capsule, without the benefit of much ongoing support. We barely have time to talk to friends and colleagues between sessions; during some days we barely have time to go to the bathroom with a packed schedule.

There are also aspects of therapeutic work that have become institutionalized as standard practices even though there is little, if any, legitimate evidence for this (Kottler & Balkin, 2020). What is so sacred about the 50-minute hour? What other health professional decides ahead of time the exact dosage of treatment before even meeting the client/patient, much less studying their condition, assessing their complaints, and individualizing a plan to best serve their needs? Does *every* client require one hour of conversation each week to optimize their "cure"? Is a 90-minute scheduled initial intake interview sufficient and best for everyone who walks in the door? These are just a few of the questions that come to mind when we consider how limited we are in the ways we operate, beginning and ending sessions the same way, even sitting in the same place each time.

Although the demands of the job, and nature of one's discipline and specialty, limit the nature of what we can accomplish in our helping efforts, we are also restrained by our own demons, unresolved personal issues, and personality traits. We can blame the nature of the job, frustrations with the agency or organization, uncooperative clients, and insensitive administrators or supervisors, but ultimately most of our difficulties with stress and self-care relate to our own personal challenges.

CHAPTER 4

Personal Stressors and Challenges

An investigative reporter decided to explore the question that many wonder about, whether mental health experts have more emotional problems than the "civilian" population (Adams, 2012). There's good reason to think this idea is absurd, considering our training, expertise, and experience healing and helping others. And yet there is that belief floating around, based on an observation of a crazy "shrink" of one's acquaintance. Not only is that guy kind of strange but then there's another doctor lady who can't seem to keep her marriage together, or that mean dude who is supposedly an expert on addiction but he smokes like a fiend and is morbidly obese.

Perhaps it seems inevitable that professionals exposed to the most disturbed, disruptive, and bizarre individuals will be negatively impacted by their behavior. These people have such sad, tragic stories to tell, haunting tales of terrifying maladies or misfortune. They display personality traits that can most generously be described as a bit disturbing. They engage in terribly self-defeating, sometimes peculiar behaviors that are quite disturbing. About half of practicing therapists are threatened with violence at some point, and 40% are actually physically attacked. One third of therapists will lose a client to suicide. And we are called upon not only to listen to these tales of woe but to fix them—and do it quickly. No wonder we feel under the gun. And no surprise that the work can drive us a little crazy.

Physicians generally have higher levels of stress, depression, and suicidal ideation than the general population. To highlight one specialty within medicine, three quarters of psychiatrists report major anxiety symptoms during their careers, and two thirds report that at one time they were incapacitated by depression. They are also five times more likely to kill themselves compared to other doctors, and three times more likely than regular citizens. They are five times more likely to divorce their partners. Compared to other medical staff, mental health personnel are much more likely to miss work because of emotional problems. They also have a higher mortality rate because of the stressful nature of their jobs—and perhaps what attracted them to this work in the first place. Many of these statistical summaries of impairment vary according to the survey, but it is generally agreed that about 25% of nonmedical therapists (Norcross & VandenBos, 2018) and nurses (Monsalve-Reyes et al., 2018) are experiencing major symptoms of burnout at any one time—which is considerably better than most physicians, who report a rate closer to 50%. It is even considerably higher among teachers, since 40% leave the profession within five years.

These figures don't necessarily imply that helping professionals are more unstable or stressed than anyone else, even if they are subjected to considerable risks and difficulties on the job. It's just that people often have unrealistic expectations for those who are responsible for others' care, sometimes believing we have special powers—and in a sense we do! After all, we tend to be far more sensitive to emotional nuances, better able to read and interpret others' behavior, more knowledgeable and wise about the nature of personal problems, and in possession of extraordinary interpersonal skills in connecting with others. With that acknowledged, we also are far more aware of all the things that can go very wrong inside people's heads and hearts. There is a burden that we carry in this journey, and sometimes it does indeed exact a toll.

Historical Legacy
One of the things that has always made it difficult for us to admit we are struggling in our lives is the belief that this signals that we are no longer qualified or entitled to continue helping others. Certainly, forms of personal impairment or unresolved emotional wounds can compromise our effectiveness, but it isn't all that unusual that even the best among us wrestle with their own demons. Consider some of the luminaries in the field who had their fair share of problems that actually *informed* their seminal ideas, even if there were significant side effects.

Sigmund Freud, the theorist who first systematized treatment for mental disorders, complained himself about an assortment of different emotional maladies, as has been described earlier. He experienced blackouts, possibly triggered by the extraordinary amount of pressure, responsibility, and criticism he handled on a daily basis. It is likely his cocaine addiction operated as a form of self-medication for the constant stress. He also clearly had a self-destructive streak in some ways, engaging in behaviors he knew were unhealthy for him.

It is a true wonder how extraordinarily productive Freud remained as a physician, psychotherapist, lecturer, and writer considering the ways he was controlled by his addiction. But then he found a drug, cocaine, that is now well known as a simulant that produces feelings of euphoria and increased energy even though the side effects become problematic.

Another noted physician of the 19th century, William Halsted, considered the father of American surgery, was also fueled by cocaine addiction most of his life, managing to develop extraordinarily innovative advancements in medicine in spite of being so emotionally wounded and leading such a bizarre double life. Among his achievements, Halsted completed the first successful gallbladder surgery (on his mother on the kitchen table!) and the first successful blood transfusion (on his sister during childbirth), invented the radical mastectomy, and developed the most precise and controlled safety regimen for training other surgeons (Imber, 2011). And he did so all the while teetering on the edge of his own mental breakdown. It just goes to demonstrate how, in spite of such impairment, he managed to accomplish so much—at least until he was institutionalized.

It was also described earlier how Carl Rogers never felt truly understood during his lifetime, resorting to alcohol abuse to moderate his symptoms. At one point the pressure from his work led to a psychotic break; he believed that only Carl Whitaker could save him, but when driving down to Atlanta to consult with him, he became lost in the Smoky Mountains, where he stayed for some time until he returned home to enter therapy with one of his doctoral students (Kirschenbaum, 2008).

Most of us have witnessed a similar phenomenon among certain colleagues who appear barely able to manage the basics of their own lives and yet still produce decent outcomes in their therapeutic work. It is a mystery that is still confounding.

So many prominent theorists developed their seminal ideas as a result of their own unresolved issues and personal demons. Existentialist Viktor Frankl was all about finding meaning in suffering after surviving concentration camps and wondering how he was singled out for rescue. Erik Erikson conceived of identity development throughout the lifespan as a major life force. He never knew his father and became obsessed with his own personal identity. He even chose his own last name, declaring that he was his own singular identity. As he struggled with his own aging issues, he revised his theory to include the struggles of later maturity.

Abraham Maslow felt utterly controlled by his parents throughout his childhood. He was told what to study, who he could marry, and which career pathway he should choose, but defied his family in order to pursue his own self-actualization. That became the heart of his theory.

Alfred Adler almost died from pneumonia at age 5, leaving him weak and feeling inferior throughout his childhood. He then developed a theory of compensation for disabilities through overachievement, the hallmark of his own drive throughout his life.

Aaron Beck and Albert Ellis, the two most prominent cognitive theorists, both felt little control during their early lives, and determined to use logic, analytic reasoning, and rational thinking to overcome their fears and feelings of inadequacy. By contrast, R. D. Laing glorified and celebrated mental illness as just another form of creativity and individuality, while he slowly fell apart in his own mental deterioration.

Boris Cyrulnik developed a theory of how our history does not determine our fate, that resilience to trauma was possible no matter how much one suffered. This became his personal mission, given the trajectory of his own traumatic life. His parents died in the Auschwitz concentration camp before he was arrested and sent to the camps himself. He eventually managed to escape his fate but spent the rest of his life making sense of what he experienced, similar to Victor Frankl.

Robert Zajonc's story is even more dramatic. He was one of the founders of the social psychology of genocide and racism. He had also fled the Nazis into Poland as a child, where his parents were killed by a bomb. He was eventually discovered and arrested by the Nazis and sent to a concentration camp, where he was one of two prisoners who managed to escape. He walked 200 miles to France, after which he was captured once again before he escaped a second time. Clearly the experiences of all these men left indelible impressions that shaped the direction of their professional lives and their favored theories, which related directly to their own life experiences.

In each of these cases, there's little doubt that the individuals suffered their own disabilities, impediments, and weaknesses, yet they also found ways to compensate for them and, in many ways, their own suffering and personal struggles allowed them to better connect with others who were also having problems. Rather than see them as indications of shame and weakness, they converted their own traumas into signature strengths and evidence of their own resilience.

What Is Most Stressful?

It is not the intention of this book to romanticize or glorify early trauma as the engine of achievement in our field, but rather to highlight the ways that some distinguished professionals have managed to recover from stress and use their own personal struggles as motivating forces. This only works, of course, if we are truly honest about the nature and depth of our challenges, acknowledging them as potential impediments if we are unwilling or unable to work them through.

No matter how resilient, well-trained, and prepared we might be, there are still particular kinds of clinical experiences that professionals say push them over the edge and test them beyond their capabilities. Although stress and burnout typically build slowly over time, there are sometimes specific incidents or circumstances that finally bring attention to the extent of the difficulties. In some other cases, the extreme stress can result from being caught off guard or just not ready to handle certain kinds of situations or individuals presenting rather extreme or dramatic behavior. A dramatic example of this occurred during the pandemic in which the actual COVID-19 virus wasn't the only thing that became so contagious. Health providers on the front line were forced to not only risk their health, but also their emotional well-being because of a sense of helplessness. The repercussions and trauma will continue for many years, requiring an unprecedented level of self-care that hasn't been needed since the last Depression or World War.

Clients Who Drive Us Crazy

These extreme sources of stress can conveniently be divided into several distinct categories beyond those caused by catastrophes, and the one that is mentioned most often relates to complaints about so-called difficult clients, those we believe to be obstructive, disobedient, challenging, manipulative, or otherwise resistant in some way. These are the clients who act out in dramatic ways. They may be wildly unpredictable, uncooperative, or dramatic in their behavior. They engage in hopelessly self-defeating behavior, unwilling to accept any responsibility for their predicaments; they tend to blame others, including our feeble efforts to help them, as a continued source of their misery. They trigger our own sense of helplessness, discouragement, and inadequacy, since it feels like nothing we might do with these clients has the slightest enduring impact.

It's interesting how the kinds of cases that therapists mention in this regard tend to vary a bit, depending on personal preferences, specialties, and interests. Cited most frequently are clients who present chronic forms of mental illness, stable personality disorders, or rather severe depression or anxiety. Many therapists also mention they are triggered by clients who are overly accusatory or manipulative, those who are suicidal risks, or who are so enmeshed in toxic peer or family dynamics that it appears almost nothing could put a dent in their behavior. These kinds of cases not only increase our stress, but also lead to questioning our very competence.

During a time in my life when I was "toast," totally burned out by my work, I had this great idea for a book that would be called *Clients from Hell*. Each chapter would be about a specific kind of client sent from hell to make my life miserable (Kottler, 1992a). There was the adolescent who would tell me to "go fuck myself" whenever I asked him a question, the client who wouldn't talk at all no matter what I said or did, or the one who rambled constantly about superficial topics to avoid any meaningful engagement. Then there was the one who dutifully came to sessions regularly but never appeared to change significantly. There were clients who continuously lied, those who were manipulative, controlling, non-compliant, resistant, challenging, abusive, and so on. One of the reviewers of the book suggested I might have a problem in that I seemed to have lost my compassion, which was indeed the case. I was blaming my clients for being difficult when, in fact, I was the one with the problem.

Nevertheless, we hear our colleagues—or ourselves—complain frequently about certain clients who are so uncooperative or toxic that they drive us crazy. They demand instant results, but they don't appear willing to make the most simple changes that would offer them some relief. In some ways they enjoy the power and control that accompanies getting under our skin.

Climate and Culture

After resistant, uncooperative, or hateful clients, practitioners cite their work environment as the next most problematic aspect of their jobs. This can range from being poorly compensated to feeling disrespected and unsupported. It can involve the physical space being inadequate or uncomfortable, or the organizational culture that seems poisonous because of interpersonal conflicts, supervisory neglect, or just scant resources. One of the most extreme examples of this relates to a group of psychiatry residents I supervised who were forced to do shifts in the emergency rooms of the county hospitals during the Covid-19 pandemic but were not supplied with adequate protective gear and were operating way outside of their expertise.

It's also interesting that, when studies of stressful work environments are conducted, what appears to most contribute to burnout are factors that have little to do with the job itself and are more related to the commute to work, the pressures to meet productivity quotas (number of billable hours or client sessions), evaluative processes by supervisors, and the person's own reluctance to take time off because of fears he or she would fall further behind (Bloom, 2020). Thus cities like Los Angeles and Chicago are rated the most stressful in the United States because of the long commute times and excessive hours that people work. Tokyo, Mumbai, and Seoul are ranked the most stressful cities in the world, not because of the nature of the work, but because people work so many hours without vacations or recovery time.

Regardless of the city of residence, clinicians most often mention their time pressures, how they are required to complete work tasks or responsibilities within parameters that are neither realistic nor particularly healthy. Perhaps because of limited funding or poorly allocated budgets, it feels like we might be expected to do more and more with so much less support. For those who work in public agencies, the pressure from waiting lists and excessive caseload contributes to overwhelming stress; for many in private practice, it may be the opposite scenario—constant worry that new referrals will stop coming or that holes in the schedule will never be filled.

In almost every industry, workers complain about excessive meetings that are boring and a waste of time. Within some agencies and organizations, even if intentions are legitimate in order to include staff in more transparent decision making, many supervisors and administrators are simply unskilled at leading group gatherings. The meetings go on far too long, or some participants are permitted to dominate and control the proceedings to the exclusion of the many others who are (or feel) marginalized. Some leaders present endless slide presentations and persist in their monologues even though it is clear to anyone who is paying attention that everyone is checked out. Participants are playing with their phones, bored and yawning, restless and constantly counting the minutes until they can get back to work and the crushing tasks that await them.

There could also be systemic dysfunctions within the organization in which rules and regulations present intrinsic conflicts between the desire to serve clients versus the needs of the agency to generate income, fill schedules, or meet some quantitative outcomes. The classic example of this is being limited by policy or rules in the number of sessions allowed, or the kind of treatment to be administered, even though that is hardly in clients' best interests. If staff are required to share an office, or fight for space, that can also be problematic at times. In addition, one of the most frequent complaints among health providers is that they are not consulted on policies by administrators but simply ordered to function in particular ways that seem senseless or inefficient or not in the best interests of their patients.

Within the larger animal kingdom (or queendom) there is clear evidence of the ways that hierarchical power differentials create the greatest stress levels among a species. For example, the life of subordinate female rhesus macaque monkeys is not much fun considering how often they are dominated, harassed, marginalized, and abused by males with the most power. They often develop body shakes, nervous pacing, excessive scratching and grooming behaviors, and startle responses. In addition, their reproductive systems become disrupted during times of extreme anxiety related to their "jobs" because it doesn't feel safe to produce offspring (Moskowitz, 2008).

There are obvious parallels in the human work environment, in which those without power or control over their time and assigned tasks tend to experience the most severe stress levels. That is one reason why Amazon warehouse employees have 100% turnover every year; they just can't maintain the inhumane expectations of management to meet their assigned quotas.

The environment can also present rather stressful circumstances if it doesn't feel safe or if the referrals directed your way don't match with your interests and skill set. Let's face it: We have sometimes been required to take positions out of obligation, or even desperation, even though they don't really fit with our preferences.

Personal Stressors

It's pretty obvious that the greatest stressors affecting our jobs don't necessarily arise from the work itself as much as from what we are dealing with in our personal lives. We tell our clients all the time that so much of their suffering is self-induced, determined by how they process and interpret their experiences. We are hardly immune from our own faulty thinking, unrealistic expectations, and unresolved issues that interfere with our ability to be more forgiving of our own limitations. If we hold perfectionistic standards we can never reach, it dooms us to disappointment. If we are desperately afraid of failure then we continually function in self-protective ways that limit personal and professional effectiveness. We would be reluctant to take constructive risks, experiment with new strategies, and accept responsibility for mistakes we might make.

If we are encountering relationship conflicts with family, partners, colleagues, or others, this is going to have a significant impact on our mood and sense of equanimity. If we have structured a less than healthy lifestyle related to diet, exercise, habits, addictions, and life balance, we are not going to function at our best. If we fail to address our own emotional difficulties, there is likely to be some collateral damage in other areas.

Impairment is an awfully strong word to use when describing any person's functioning, especially when that person is a helping professional. Most of us have learned quite well from our training and have been able to shore up our defenses. We are an adaptable group, by and large. We are also quite good at presenting ourselves to others in the best possible light. This posture is quite necessary to instill in others confidence and trust in us.

Nevertheless, for many of us the question is not *whether* we are impaired but *to what extent* we are impaired at this particular moment. Each of us struggles on a daily basis with our own unresolved issues that may or may not interfere with our personal and professional functioning. This is not only about gross dysfunctions such as addiction, depression, or personality disorders. Rather, in this context impairment is defined as any of the qualities, behaviors, or attitudes that somehow compromise maximum effectiveness—as a human being and as a professional.

Treadway (2020) has noted that 80% of the therapists he has surveyed admit that some unresolved issue or trauma from their childhood was a primary motivation for becoming a therapist in the first place. That is why he considers it so important that "part of being a healer is to have our own centering practice, in which we connect our small insignificant lives to a pattern of meaning in the universe in whatever way we understand it" (p. 58). This, he insists, allows us not only to remain sane in the face of the craziness we encounter every day, but also to keep our composure and humility while we deal with client suffering without further wounding ourselves.

Each of us is haunted by the past in some way. We all have unresolved issues. Most of us walk around feeling wounded at least some of the time and do our mighty best to pretend that everything is just fine. But what if you could let the veil down for a few minutes?

It's a bit unnerving to reflect on some of the same questions we might ask our clients:

- What haunts you the most and plagues with memories of failure, defeat, and not being good enough?
- In what ways are you less than fully functioning and feel limited by some of your weaknesses?
- What are some aspects of your lifestyle that are unhealthy?
- In what ways do you "medicate" yourself during times of stress?
- What are some of the lies you tell yourself that permit you to function in compromised ways?
- What are you hiding from and what do you most wish to avoid?
- Who gets to you most and what is it about those interactions that trigger you in undesirable ways?
- What is it about these questions that you find most threatening?

In general, there are obvious differences in the propensity to experience severe stress and burnout depending on the work setting and our own chosen attitudes. Those who feel a sense of autonomy and control over their schedule and practices are much less likely to report difficulties, which is one reason why those in the public sector may be more vulnerable than private practitioners. Other predictors of trouble relate to youth and inexperience, since over time veterans learn how to conserve their energy, moderate their expectations, and better regulate their emotional responses (McCormack et al., 2018).

Professional Lapses, Biases, and Blind Spots

Although the nature of your job, the people you work with, and the settings you work in supply some of the stressors in your life, pressure also emanates from the particular strengths and weaknesses of your clinical style. As hard as you try to be helpful to your clients, you face personal and professional limitations on a daily basis. Furthermore, you confront your own lapses in knowledge, execution, and thinking. There isn't a session you've ever conducted about which you can't think of at least a dozen things you could have done differently or of a few issues that you wished you had handled in another way.

Whichever theoretical orientation or therapeutic approach that you prefer, there are particular times, cases, and situations when you may feel limited or handicapped. Whether identified as a psychodynamic, cognitive, constructivist, feminist, or any other kind of therapy practitioner, there are both strengths and limitations to the approach. An existential therapist consistently searches for meaning making processes, regardless of whether that is the client's major priority. A relational cultural therapist, emotionally focused therapist, or narrative therapist each search for the issues, content, and focus that is most compatible with their worldview and values. Yet no matter which model most appeals to us, especially if it is employed exclusively, there will be some clients who are not necessarily served as the best candidates.

Even within the umbrella of any single therapeutic approach, there are wide variations in a practitioner's ability to apply the methods to given cases. There are differences in training and preparation, as well as mastery of the basic skills and interventions. There are distinctions between the ways each of us interprets and applies the core ideas, depending on our personality, style, and priorities. Even within the same school of thought, we might each conceptualize the significant features of a case in radically different ways. We are hardly clones of one another, subject to individual and unique characteristics and biases. Likewise, we tend to miss certain things and home in on others, depending on personal preferences and professional imperatives.

Consider some of your own weaknesses and blind spots, what things you don't do particularly well in many situations. I struggle with impatience at times. I become bored easily and like to shake things up to keep the momentum moving—whether my clients are on board or not with this plan. I push too fast, too hard, at times. I stir things up, reluctantly admitting I do this for curiosity or entertainment value on occasion. I hate incessant whining and complaining and so have little tolerance if people tend to go on too long about all the things they don't like or wish were different. I've been known to suggest that certain clients take a break from sessions, or perhaps try to refer them to someone else, if I'm not sufficiently engaged. This is tough to admit, but if I'm truly honest I just can't help everyone I'd like. Neither can you.

There are also specific clinical challenges or therapeutic situations in which each of us excels or sometimes falls short. Some therapists aren't very diligent about establishing and enforcing boundaries, or tend to avoid conflict and confrontation, or have a hard time with clients presenting particular issues—addictions, toxic relationships, procrastination, or toxic personality styles. Some of us like to delve into the past while others prefer to stick with the present moment. We each have different tolerances for uncertainty and confusion. "I became a therapist in the first place," one therapist reveals, "because I wanted the illusion of certainty, truth, and understanding. I wanted to simplify the complexity and ambiguity of my own life and so was initially attracted to therapies that were extremely regimented, systematic, and concrete. I still struggle with honoring the mysteries of life and the complexity of human behavior without the need to reduce them to simple (but faulty) assumptions."

We thus experience increased stress on the job because of our own stubbornness and rigid preferences for what we do and how we do it. We lose focus at times, find it hard to remain fully present. We lapse into fantasies with some clients, finding it challenging to listen to their rambling, incoherent narratives. What percentage of the time would *you* estimate that you are actually fully and completely present in sessions? I have been asking this question to hundreds of therapists over the years, curious about what others would say. I have heard estimates ranging from one quarter to three quarters of the time although I think even 50% is generous, especially with some individuals who are notorious for constantly repeating themselves and telling the same stories over and over and over again. Of course there are some clients with whom we remain riveted almost all the time because their stories are so compelling or we are so engaged in the relationship. Yet there are others with whom we are barely present; we check out and just nod into a stupor, checking the clock every few minutes and amazed so little time has elapsed.

It is precisely our own hazardous attitudes or work habits that create the most self-inflicted difficulties. Those who demonstrate traits of arrogance and omnipotence, that they know it all and they've seen it all before, are going to be disappointed a lot—at least if they are paying close attention to how others respond. Clinicians who take themselves too seriously, who are desperate for constant validation, who need to be right all the time, who inflate their own self-importance, who demand that they are always in full control, are inevitably going to have problems.

In spite of advancements in theoretical, technical, methodological, and strategic aspects of our profession, leading to increased effectiveness within briefer periods of time, the pressures, stress, and neglect of self-care are becoming far worse during these challenging times. It is important that we are as scrupulously honest and direct with ourselves about the difficulties we encounter on a daily basis as we are with those we help. Any attempt to take better care of ourselves will fail miserably if we are not clear about the specific lapses, blind spots, biases, and unresolved personal issues that continue to get in our way.

CHAPTER 5

Why Things Are Becoming Worse

The vast majority of Americans report that their daily stress levels are becoming significantly worse in recent times. The current political climate, environmental decay, economic uncertainty, pandemic scares, prevalence of "fake news," and perceived dwindling resources all contribute to the pessimistic outlooks. Although personal stressors in the workplace and home continue to be factors for half the population, recent surveys have indicated that more global political and social factors are making things considerably worse (American Psychological Association, 2019). Among the concerns that are significantly magnifying pressures among our clients, as well as within our professional responsibilities, are events that feel way beyond our control. The Coronavirus pandemic and protests against racial inequality are just a few examples of events that led to massive anxiety, stress, depression, and a sense of helplessness in people's lives.

Table 5.1 reveals the percentage of the American population that feels overstressed and discouraged by several issues, dominated by fears of violence and the collapse of social structures. Such surveys were undertaken prior to the world economy shut down during the pandemic of 2020 in which millions of people lost their jobs, became seriously ill, and had to live under the harsh conditions of isolation and uncertainty about the future

Table 5.1 SOCIAL/POLITICAL SOURCES OF STRESS (PRIOR TO 2020)

Mass shootings	71%
Healthcare costs and accessibility	69%
Climate change	56%
Political elections and stability	52%
Immigration	48%
Racism and discrimination	25%

There is a new diagnosis identified by health professionals, called "headline stress disorder," that has been having a major impact on people of all political convictions (Daspin, 2019; Stosny, 2019). Increasingly, people are feeling overwhelmed and worn out by the news, affecting almost everyone. It is no wonder, considering that one in ten individuals admit to checking the news every hour for updates.

Regardless of one's personal problems and pressures, the whole structural fabric of the social/political landscape feels like it is fracturing. A vast majority of citizens say that this is the "lowest point in our nation's history" and the "future of our nation" is at risk (Ramsey, 2018)—and that was even before the world economies crashed, unemployment skyrocketed, and even basic necessities like toilet paper and soap became difficult to secure. The increased stress about political news first began during the Bush administration but was multiplied significantly during the Trump era, with people questioning the integrity and competence of the country's leaders, the reliability of the news media, and the meaning of fake news during a time when the president had been found to lie or misstate facts tens of thousands of times. Many people lost faith in their government's ability to provide needed support and care during times of crises, making *self*-care even more critical.

New Challenges in Contemporary Life

If headline news has exacerbated and increased stress then we also have to add to the equation the impact of social media in which people are constantly making comparisons between themselves and others, often feeling shortchanged in some way. One major source of stress results from the tendency to measure our own success and achievements according to what we believe is true for others (Shensa et al., 2020). It's been found that those who spend the most time connected to social media are often at highest risk for depression and anxiety (Shensa et al., 2018). It's no wonder when we consider the kinds of messages that people project on their personal sites, projecting images of themselves supposedly enjoying life to its fullest. Rarely does anyone post announcements about how much they hate their jobs, how they were brutally rejected by a romantic interest, when they are feeling so blue they can hardly get out of bed, or how empty their lives feel.

Although, ironically, social media was designed to increase interpersonal engagement, it often results in feelings of greater isolation and dissatisfaction, especially since it leads to constant comparisons between one's triumphs, satisfactions, and prizes compared to others. If you feel great that your practice is filled four days a week, but then learn that your colleagues are busy with five days of clients, then the satisfaction can feel tarnished. Such is the case with any other life experience, achievement, or object of desire.

To add to the pressures, our culture rewards and idealizes busyness with status and admiration. It is a sign of success and self-importance. Lawyers boast about the number of billable hours they log in a week. There is an anecdote in a Grisham novel in which a character brags that he managed to bill 27 hours in a single day by flying from the East Coast to the West Coast (adding three hours because of the time change) without taking a break from his responsibilities. Likewise medical residents compete with one another about how many consecutive hours they are on call without sleep. Teachers, counselors, and psychotherapists are also known to compete with one another on a "martyr scale" to demonstrate their personal sacrifices and commitment to their profession. Most of the measures of success in our culture—a fancy car, expensive wardrobe, social media "likes"—are considered badges of value and self-worth.

There are important historical reasons for encouraging citizens to work hard on behalf of the greater good. During ancient times, laziness and sloth were potentially dangerous to the tribe if everyone didn't pitch in and do their fair share of the work to gather food, build shelter, and protect against enemies or predators. Of course, this was only during crises and times of hardship, since the average workweek during the hunter-gatherer era was less than 20 hours; the rest of the time was reserved for hanging out, socializing, and napping.

These days there is no longer even just an 8-hour work day or 40-hour work week, with the constant access to communication with anyone or everyone who might want a piece of you. Clients, colleagues, or supervisors can text you during all hours of the day and night, fully expecting a response within hours, regardless of whether you are still on duty.

Radical advances in technology each decade only add to the stress of con-temporary life. Every few months there are software updates to our devices, requiring us to learn new procedures and tricks when the old ones seemed to work just fine. A mobile device is considered obsolete after just a few years, requiring the purchase of a new one that is infinitely more powerful but also more complicated to operate with all the new bells and whistles. There once was a time when the only technological skill needed was to change the ribbon on a typewriter or replace the tape in an answering machine. Now it is an exercise in frustration just to figure out how to fill out all the online forms and get them to behave properly when we click "send."

As history has shown us again and again, there are unintended consequences to these innovations and advancements. The invention of agriculture and domes-ticated animals is one such example, designed to provide more stable, convenient, accessible food supplies, but at a terrible cost (Diamond, 2005). Prior to that we were hunter-gatherers with constantly changing food choices depending what was available in the area. Certainly there were periods of deprivation and scarcity, which is why it seemed so wonderful that we could just walk out to a barn, stockyard, or garden and retrieve whatever we wished.

Unfortunately, once we remained in place, in close proximity to cows, goats, pigs, and chickens, we were susceptible to their diseases. Hundreds of millions among our species have since perished from the Black Plague, tuberculosis, typhus, diphtheria, measles, influenza, leprosy, viruses, and other horrible diseases contracted from the animals we intended to eat. In fact, 60% of all contagious or infectious diseases that afflict humans are the result of close contact with domestic animals (Bryson, 2019). Likewise, our overreliance on food staples that were convenient and accessible, like grains, has led to nutritional deficiencies that are the result of a much less varied diet. Diseases like diabetes, food allergies, structural skeletal pain (back and neck), obesity, and other health problems are the result of three radical changes in cultural evolution that began with the agricultural revolution and industrial revolution, and continue at an accelerated pace with the technological revolution that operates at a blazing speed with which our bodies and minds can never quite keep up (Lieberman, 2013).

It is ironic that with all the scientific advances and medical discoveries of the past century, life expectancy has doubled, yet the quality of daily life may not have been much improved, considering that half of elderly people live with major disabilities or chronic pain. The average length of retirement that people enjoyed 50 years ago was only about eight years; today it can last two or three decades. This means that self-care for stress—and its opposite condition, boredom—will only continue to increase in importance as people scramble for ways to manage these challenges and especially to find meaning in their final years of life.

Misguided Assumptions

Physicians focus mostly on their own interventions to fix stress-related diseases and health issues, usually well after the symptoms are out of control. Rather than emphasizing ways that people can prevent such problems in the first place, the medical profession continues to rely on a model that neglects healthy lifestyle habits related to diet, sleep, and work schedule, even though these factors account for up to 70% of the influences that can lead to major chronic diseases. There appears to be a major disconnect between the beliefs of doctors and their patients, sometimes to a ridiculous and disturbing degree. A dramatic example of this from a historical perspective is illustrated in a 1960s a survey, which determined that 85% of cancer patients insisted that they wanted to know if they were dying, yet close to 90% of their physicians refused to inform them of their terminal status, believing it would just bring them more discomfort and suffering (Oken, 1961).

In more recent studies, 97% of physicians say that self-care is a critical part of healthcare, although half of them say that their patients are just not interested in taking on such responsibility. This is in direct contrast to 75% of patients who say they have never once discussed *any* aspect of self-care with their doctors in the previous two years. Perhaps one reason for this is that the majority of physicians say they don't have time to address their own stress-related problems and practice basic self-care (Jonas, 2019).

The discrepancy between doctor and patient perceptions is also played out in the relationships that take place in psychotherapy, since there is a similar misunderstanding in what is believed to be most helpful. Although therapists consistently point to their own interventions, theoretical preferences, and favored techniques as what makes the greatest difference in their work, clients more frequently mention that they felt heard and understood (Kottler & Balkin, 2017, 2020).

In another example of the misguided excuses and reasons why people say they don't take better care of themselves and deal with the disruptive stress in their lives, they either just don't have enough time or they can't afford to do so because they believe they would have to spend a lot of money. Clearly this is not really the case, considering that most of the choices could become habituated over time without much time or expense involved.

Among all the predictors of future difficulty with work stress and failing self-care efforts, it is our personal characteristics, interpersonal style, attitudes, beliefs, and expectations that are most significant. There are several personal characteristics (conscientiousness, dependability, commitment, sociability) that ultimately determine our ability to maintain a healthier lifestyle.

Many of us entered the profession in the first place not just to save the world but also, in some sense, to save ourselves. We are do-gooders who genuinely care about others and desperately want to make a difference in their lives. And yet we are often disappointed. Clients don't necessarily want to get better, at least in the same ways that we think would be best. And those who genuinely are committed and highly motivated may still test our patience through their self-defeating patterns and self-sabotage. Whatever idealism, optimism, and altruism we might have once felt is continually tested by successive disappointments and failures.

Litany of Fears

(It is one of our most closely guarded secrets that we don't know nearly as much as we pretend, and understand much less than we would ever admit.)A new client enters the office and presents a complex configuration of symptoms and a host of problems that have lasted a lifetime. While we furiously take notes and nod our heads in acknowledgment, there is a voice inside our heads that is screaming in panic.

"Holy crap! I have no idea what this person is talking about and no clue what any of this means."

Of course we just smile reassuringly and cue the person to keep talking, hoping eventually we can grab onto a thread that may lead to a glimpse of what might be going on. No matter how long we've been practicing, how much experience we've logged or training and supervision we've received, the reality is that some (most?) of the time we are confused and lost. Interestingly, this doesn't seem to matter very much in the process. It seems that as long as the client sees that we are listening carefully, and *appear* to understand the gist of what he or she is saying, that is sufficient to keep things moving forward.

There are all kinds of publicly unacknowledged fears that can paralyze us and undermine both our credibility and sense of efficacy. There is the *fear of rejection* that is often triggered by the client who doesn't return without explanation. It seemed like everything was proceeding quite smoothly according to the plan but then the sessions just abruptly end and we are left to wonder what happened and why. Did we do something wrong? Did we somehow offend the person? Or maybe the outcome was already satisfactory? More often than not, we may be inclined to blame ourselves for some misdeed.

If the fear of rejection is case specific, then the more general dread is a *fear of failure.* I've made a whole career out of talking about concerns related to the mistakes I've made, the miscalculations, the awkward or mistimed attempts to be helpful that just fell flat (Kottler & Blau, 1989; Kottler & Balkin, 2020; Kottler & Carlson, 2002, 2011; Kottler, 2018). This is the most insidious and chronic form of self-doubt that often drives the futile search for perfectionism that will always be out of reach. Such mistakes, failures, and disappointments can also represent some of our most critical lessons and professional growth. In his study of how physicians think and make sense of their patients' reported maladies, Groopman (2008) describes a colleague who kept a meticulous record throughout his distinguished career of every single mistake, error in judgment, and misdiagnosis that he made so that he might learn better learn from these experiences. There is, thus, a balance to be attained between scrupulous honesty regarding our failures and acceptance of our own limitations.

A corollary to fearing failure is the *fear of ineptitude,* the core feeling of inadequacy that transcends mere professional competence to include the personal realm. There is a feeling of never knowing enough, never being able to do enough, never feeling prepared enough, never being well trained enough. No matter how hard we study and work, how many degrees we accumulate, how many workshops and seminars we attend, how much supervision we receive, there is still considerable doubt that all of this still leaves us lacking in some way. And yet, once again, it is precisely the willingness to acknowledge our mistakes that ultimately improves our performance. "Studies show that expertise is largely acquired not only by sustained practice but by receiving feedback that helps you understand your technical errors and misguided decisions (Groopman, 2008, p. 21).

It is when making constant comparisons to others that feelings of ineptitude can lead to the *fear of mediocrity*. In spite of the pronouncement that three-quarters of clinicians believe (or say they believe) they are more skilled and competent than their colleagues, we are sometimes left to wonder whether, somehow, we are really barely better than average. We may strive for excellence and extraordinary achievement but at times we may settle for a degree of complacency and modest results.

On the other side of the coin, rather than lamenting some lack of potency we may hold a *fear of power*. Clients sometimes worship and deify us, believing we hold some superpower or secret to immortality—or at least exalted existence. In one sense they aren't far wrong in that we *do* know and understand meaningful insights that lead to increased well-being. And yet there are times when we might offer some throw-away line or do something that appears insignificant and benign, watching in horror as the client takes it the wrong way and becomes offended or furious. Our job requires that we make benevolent use of power to influence others and yet there are times that we feel terrified by this responsibility.

There is a *fear of limitations* related to what is truly realistic given our restricted role and opportunities in someone's life, especially when there are all kinds of toxic influences at play. On some level we realize how futile it sometimes seems to talk to someone for an hour each week, thinking this will really matter, when we know full well they are returning to the same dysfunctional family or peer group that may inevitably undermine and sabotage any progress. This particular concern leads to a *fear of shattered illusions,* a far deeper and more existential sense of doubt in which we wonder whether we are really helping anyone with our rather modest attempts to cure suffering with conversation. When we compare the options within our standard repertoire to those of physicians, who have at their disposal all kinds of technological, neurological, surgical, pharmacological, and fancy diagnostic hardware (even blood tests or genetic markers!) we are left to wonder what kind of difference we really make in people's lives.

The last fears to be mentioned are triggered by even more personal vulnerabilities. There is the *fear of losing control,* whether being seduced by a client, or just losing our composure in some way when subjected to a high degree of manipulation or deception. After all, trust works in both directions in therapeutic relationships: If we don't trust a particular client we are likely to operate in very cautious, limited, and self-protective ways. An even more extreme variation is the *fear of annihilation*, especially when working with those who have very florid personality disturbances. Such individuals may attempt to penetrate our souls, manipulate and control us, attempt to knock us off our pedestals as a way to bolster their own sense of powerlessness.

Finally, last but perhaps most common of all, is the *fear of complacency* when the job starts to feel predictable, tedious, even boring at times. It feels like some of our clients start to sound the same. It may seem like we've stopped learning much that is all that novel or different. This often signals the first stages of burnout or rustout, when passion is reduced as we slip into the routines of the job.

Although it might seem like stress problems at work result exclusively from an individual's laziness, complacency, incompetence, neglect, or negative attitude (all of which are certainly factors), it may be far more accurate to place the blame on the organizational culture and environment that allows such behavior among staff to continue. It's not as if administrators and supervisors aren't aware there are such difficulties; in some cases it might very well be *their* stress and burnout that is affecting everyone else!

In certain settings, other staff may feel like rivals and competitors rather than true colleagues who have your back. When compensation or value is measured according to certain rubrics that track billable hours, number of clients treated, and other outcome measures, a culture can be created that minimizes mutual support and cooperation.

Failure to Enforce Limits on Ourselves and Boundaries With Others

We're supposed to be experts at setting and enforcing boundaries. We do this to protect our clients from exploitation and our own self-serving and self-indulgent desires, but also to protect ourselves from excessive burdens. When he first developed the first form of psychotherapy, Freud considered it imperative that clear and consistent parameters were enforced without exception. Of course he put his patients on the couch not only to facilitate free association but because he didn't like them staring at him all day. He was also concerned about protection from his own sexual temptations with mostly attractive, vulnerable females within his care. With that said, Freud still insisted on experimenting with alternatives that increased the likelihood of lapses, since he would some-times go for a walk with a patient or agree to consult with someone who was an acquaintance, colleague, or friend.

There are boundaries and limits most of us establish with regard to time parameters, fee payments, and modes of communication. Some professionals respond to queries during all hours of the day and night while others have strict limits they enforce consistently. Some professionals set limits with regard to the types of clients they will agree to treat, depending on the type and severity of the problems or the extent to which the persons are perceived to be challenging.

Some professionals don't have the discretion or power to control their own schedules. They are required to see anyone who walks in the door. They are scheduled a certain number of clients within a day or week, regardless of the cases, specialties, circumstances, or context. For those in private practice, there is often a self-inflicted burden in that it's hard to turn away any new referral, regardless of how busy you might already be, especially when your livelihood depends on the reliable income.

Regardless of the work setting, and excuses offered, almost everyone has the ability to structure their workdays with some discretion, scheduling breaks as needed, refusing to go beyond reasonable limits. There are also so many options with respect to the ways we might function and operate professionally, whether it is adjusting the manner, style, or kind of treatment approach we employ. The practice of therapy can be, and should be, a creative enterprise in spite of the pressure to provide consistent, reliable, evidence-based, empirically sanctioned methods. It is when we get stuck in familiar routines and comfortable patterns that we sometimes limit the opportunities to access greater passion and innovation.

Perhaps the most important boundary and limit-setting of all has to do with our investment and (over)involvement in clients' lives. This is, in fact, the single best predictor of burnout—that is, caring too damn much to the point that we lose a sense of personal control (Lee et al., 2011). We can't stop thinking about certain clients. We take on board their suffering. We worry about them to the point that it affects our own emotional stability—and distracts us from our own personal issues that we may be hiding from.

It is understandable and perfectly normal that we worry about some of our clients, patients, students, and supervisees. It is not so much that we do so because we believe that such concerns are actually helpful to them, but rather because we care so much about their welfare. During the week we might wonder how they are doing or reflect on things we might talk about during the next session. We also relive aspects of our conversations over and over to figure out how we might make a greater difference.

Additional perspective on this overinvestment and overinvolvement in client welfare can be found in the ways that we feel so strongly connected to fictional characters in favorite shows or films. Mirror neurons in our brain make it possible for us to feel such empathic engagement with figures in stories that it very much feels like they are dear friends we care about deeply. And in a sense they are! We worry about what will happen to certain characters next, are moved to tears by their trials and tribulations and traumas, and feel connections to them that seem to rival anything we feel toward other loved ones. This might seem peculiar but it a gift that evolution provided to us so that we might accumulate experiences vicariously.

Yes, we become overinvested at times, even in ways that disturb our sleep, but we also have the ability to stop these rescue fantasies when they become excessive or uncomfortable. Maybe this is a rationalization, but I've never really desired to stop these "leakages" as long as they are not too disruptive. I suppose I enjoy the internal processing that takes place in which I reflect on the possible meanings of others' behavior, and try to make sense of what is happening in their lives, or in our relationship. I also must like feeling self-important, that my clients' lives depend on my dedicated commitment even when the meter isn't running. I've been challenged by supervisors in the past that perhaps I'm doing this more for myself than for others because of some emptiness or need in my life. There is some merit to this interpretation, but I still insist that occasional reflection (and concern) about my clients sometimes leads to breakthroughs, as well as new insights, growth, and learning on my part.

Whether this is an issue for you or not, the key point is knowing for each of us what we can reasonably manage—and what we cannot. There are times we've had to "fire" a particular client, or at least encourage them to go away, because they are more than we can handle. When someone becomes inordinately frustrating, complaining, pushy, and inappropriately demanding, I've heard myself suggest that perhaps they might be better off seeing someone else. I'm not especially proud of surrendering to my own impatience or intolerance, but I also recognize a few things I don't do very well. Thus setting our own limits represents a negotiation between desired goals and the realities of what is indeed possible. Like almost everything else in life, it comes down to our own beliefs and attitudes.

Monitoring Attitudes and Beliefs

McGonigal (2015) popularized the notion that it is essentially our own attitudes toward and interpretations of stress experiences that determine their eventual effects on our mind and body. She has found in her research that those who believe stress is detrimental to their health will actually have far more difficulties than those who adopt a "stress mindset" that merely interprets such events as challenging. "When you believe stress is harmful," she summarizes, "anything that feels a bit stressful can start to feel like an intrusion in your life" (p. 69).

Those with a "stress-is-enhancing" mindset tend to see such situations as potentially positive growth opportunities that heighten their focus and attention, and lead ultimately to greater satisfaction. Even more intriguing, adopting this perspective during threats and crises actually increases anabolic growth hormones that lead to faster and longer lasting recovery (Crum et al., 2017). It doesn't seem to matter much if the situation is perceived as potentially critical or dangerous as long as there is an expectation that this could be an interesting, stimulating, and exciting ride. McGonigal thus makes the point that metabolizing stress effectively doesn't mean being unbothered by the trials of life, but rather feeling inspired and motivated to take on these challenges with the expectation of gifts learned along the way.

Ultimately the key question to ask oneself during times of adversity is: Does this feel like a threat to my very survival, or else just an opportunity to rise to the occasion? The answer depends on whether it feels like you have the skills, experience, support, and resources to handle the situation or not. And if there is indeed something lacking, that is a strong signal it's time to get to work and build (or learn) whatever is most needed to immunize oneself in the future against similar predicaments.

On three successive occasions over a few recent years (I'm a slow learner) I found myself working in dire circumstances treating acute trauma after major disasters (earthquakes, floods, fires, mass shooting). With the best of intentions, and considerable overconfidence, I suffered collateral damage to my health and emotional well-being. Each time I told myself I was better prepared to handle the overwhelming stress but with little noticeable progress in this domain: I lost weight, had sleep disruptions, and experienced recurrent intrusive, disturbing memories. I wish this was an example in which I learned the necessary preparation to better immunize myself against vicarious trauma and compassionate fatigue but instead what I now accept and acknowledge is that, at this stage of life, I'm not built any longer for this kind of work that feels beyond my capability. Or at least that's what I tell myself as part of my current stress mindset that acknowledges my present limitations. As much as I "enjoy" the drama, excitement, and satisfaction of working in devastated regions of the world, I realize my own limits and weaknesses that don't permit me to emerge unscathed. I just care too damn much and can't seem to maintain firm boundaries with the desperate people I so much wish to help.

I have moved on from many different professional assignments during my life, each time recognizing that there was some mismatch between the demands of the job and my own capabilities, skill set, and genuine interests. There are many among us who fervently believe that there are far worse conditions than feeling stressed and overwhelmed—the state of boredom, complacency, and staleness in which everything is predictable and controlled. Humans thrive on novelty and stimulation in any possible form. One of our jobs is to help clients to embrace such opportunities and to expand their capacity for taking constructive risks, experimenting with new behaviors, and testing themselves in challenging circumstances. This is what builds cognitive flexibility, adaptability, resilience, and hardiness, regardless of the original presenting complaints that brought the person into treatment in the first place.

CHAPTER 6

What Hardly Ever Works and Why

I attended a lecture by a colleague who was talking about the importance of setting limits on the things in our lives that activate or increase stress. She defined self-care not so much as adding another task or activity but rather cutting down on our existing commitments and choices. This made perfect sense to me. She even had us practice declining new invitations—or demands on our time and our psyche:

> "No, I'll pass on that."
> "No *thank* you. I'm good."
> "Yes, I'm sure."

Then she asked everyone to consider something we were doing on a regular basis that we might stop doing in order to reduce stress, pressure, and discouragement. Immediately, one thing came to mind. Every morning I spend at least an hour beginning my day devouring the news. I breeze through at least a dozen different newspapers and magazines online, plus an assortment of editorials, blogs, and opinion pieces interpreting whatever depressing, annoying, discouraging, frustrating, terrible things happened the day before. It occurred to me this would be a perfect opportunity to set some limits.

Since the speaker asked us to write down something we were currently doing that we could commit to *stop* doing—*this* was a perfect candidate that would significantly reduce my own stress and daily dissatisfaction. After all, every day for me begins with digesting and metabolizing all the bad news that seems to undermine and demean what I value most.

Before you decide this is a fabulous idea that you should consider as well, I want to mention another facet of this process that is, as yet, unfinished. I looked at my commitment scribbled on a scrap of paper, feeling inordinately proud of myself. This would truly make *such* a difference in the quality of my life. I couldn't wait to test this out the very next morning. I was so proud of this takeaway from an otherwise pretty standard lecture on the subject.

The talk ended. Just like almost everyone else, I reached for my phone, first to see if anyone messaged or emailed me, then a quick scan of a social media site, eventually migrating over to a news site to see what happened with the impeachment that was unfolding at the time. But wait! Just a minute earlier I had said I wasn't going to do that anymore!

It was in that moment that I had a more powerful revelation related to this subject of self-care: What most discourages and sabotages our efforts is really not a lack of will power or motivation but rather making commitments that are neither realistic nor very practical. I realized there was no way I was going to refrain from checking the news each morning. I have too much time on my hands in the early hours and don't know what to do with myself. As much as I might complain about the effects of this choice, I also revel in the indignation. I *love* staying informed. I even get lots of cool ideas for writing projects. So what I actually had done was commit myself to a self-care strategy that was doomed to failure from the very beginning. Lesson learned: Don't say I'm going to do something when I honestly know I'm not prepared to follow through.

This is hardly a groundbreaking insight given that we tell our clients something similar during most sessions. We wisely advise them how important it is that their goals and declarations remain realistic, practical, and virtually guaranteed to be attainable.

Aspirational and Ambitious Goals

If one big mistake that leads to failure is setting goals that are realistically out of reach, the counterpoint is that it sometimes helps (in specific, optimal circumstances) to attempt aspirations that seem far beyond your capability. A colleague of mine, Sara Safari, was working with me on a project in Nepal rescuing, mentoring, and supporting at-risk girls who are at greatest risk for being forced into early marriage or sex slavery. Sara was attending a leadership workshop when everyone was asked to declare an impossible goal. The woman sitting in front of her announced the rather dramatic goal that she would trek to Everest Base Camp above 17,000 feet.

Not to be outdone, Sara impulsively blurted out that she would actually *climb* Mt. Everest! That was indeed an admirable goal given that she wanted to inspire girls in Nepal who felt so powerless and marginalized. She wanted to show them that a woman could do anything a man could do. The problem, however, was that Sara had spent her early life in Tehran and had since immigrated to southern California so she had never been in snow before, much less ever been camping. She had no climbing experience, no equipment, and no particular athletic ability. Needless to say, her initial attempts at climbing even the easiest, qualifying mountains ended in abject failure. Again and again she failed to summit and even had some near-death experiences because of her lack of preparation. Yet with persistence, training, and incredible perseverance, eventually she even broadened her goal to become the first Iranian woman to scale the Seven Summits, the highest mountain on each continent. After a series of setbacks, failures, tragedies, and life-threatening events, surviving earthquakes, avalanches, strikes, personal difficulties, and disappointments, she eventually did reach this goal and, along the way, discovered her ultimate form of self-care by taking on new challenges (Safari & Kottler, 2018).

Sara's adventures inspired me to attempt my own goals that seemed out of reach, as a means of self-care during a time in my life when I was feeling lost and invisible. I was approaching my 70th birthday, a milestone that signals retirement and disengagement. But I wasn't feeling ready to surrender quite yet. So I decided I was going to attempt to climb the two highest volcanoes in Mexico, both over 17,000 feet. The operative word in that declaration is "attempt," because my goal wasn't about the necessity of reaching the summits but rather having a structure to train for something that felt beyond my physical ability. I have climbed mountains that high in the past, but more than a decade earlier. Several of my previous climbs ended before I reached the top because of blinding snowstorms and high winds, or else just pure exhaustion. I didn't care so much about the achievement of bagging a summit; all I wanted was something to aim for.

I had conceived of this adventure as an example of a "stress challenge," one that would test me and push me to my limits, but also one that I had freely chosen. I vowed that no matter what I would not complain about the inevitable suffering since this was an intrinsic part of the experience: I willingly chose, at great expense, discomfort, and inconvenience, to take on this assignment. Predictably it was miserable—freezing temperatures (several team members became hypothermic), blowing winds, brutal conditions carrying a 65-pound pack, peeing in bottles at night to avoid leaving the tent, and ultimately, failure after deciding it just wasn't safe or possible for me to continue to the summit after reaching my limit. Lesson learned. Just like other things I shouldn't (or can't) do at my age, this is another one to check off my list.

Interestingly, I didn't feel disappointed, but rather grateful for what I learned about myself. No, that's a lie. *Of course* I was disappointed to discover another aspect of life that was now closed to me. However, in my defense, the part that was freeing in some way was accepting that although my ultimate goal was not reached, I could adapt and adjust my expectations to more realistically fit my capabilities. Aspirational self-care strategies don't have to be successful initially in order to provide structure for attempts to nourish ourselves in a multitude of ways, even when things don't work out as we hoped.

False Cures

It is probably not exactly accurate to say that some initial attempts at self-care are not effective; instead we should say that they just have some undesirable side effects. Let's be honest about this: When people find themselves overstressed and out of sorts, they typically rely on the easiest, most accessible, least taxing strategy they can think of to deal with the disruption. These might be called "false cures," but they do provide quick relief even if the results don't last and they are accompanied by unintended consequences.

The first and most common remedy for emotional discomfort is some form of biochemically soothing agent. This is not just the 20% of the population who regularly rely on prescribed antidepressant or antianxiety medications, but also those who routinely drink alcohol, ingest forms of cannabis or opiates, or take other mind-soothing substances. Then there are the other kinds of addictions that represent a life out of control—compulsive shopping or gambling, playing online or video games for hours each day (or night), spending endless hours each day binging on shows or social media. In each case, these coping strategies do provide some distraction and relief from life's stressors. The problem is that such escapist routines do nothing for the underlying problems and they do have significant dangers when used to excess.

It is clear that, when faced with discomfort and difficult circumstances, the first line of attack is to attempt to avoid the situation: Self-care thus often takes the form of escape, or at least a strategic retreat. Some people lick their wounds by isolating themselves as much as possible, preventing further damage; others do so via distractions, diversions, and self-destructive acting out.

With that said, it is also important to acknowledge that there are much healthier escapist strategies that do reduce the pressure, as well as permit recovery from daily pressures. Such routines as building deliberate, non-negotiable, strategic breaks during the day are undeniably effective, just as are scheduling time for days off, abbreviated work weeks, relaxation, social engagements, leisure time, and vacations. But even these necessary escapes can have their problems if even more work piles up during absences, requiring redoubled frantic effort to keep one's head above water.

Perhaps the most common false cure of all is the overreliance on tools, programs, apps, and books like this in order to fix problems that first require prerequisite skills. In a study of why time management tools are virtually worthless for most professionals, it was found that in order for them to work very well it is first necessary to be accurate and honest in assessing one's organizational, scheduling, and monitoring skills, most of which are found to be inadequate. Dierdorff (2020) was not surprised by these results, since it seems just as absurd that someone would order an expensive knife set and build a high-end kitchen and think this would turn him or her into a Michelin-starred chef.

In this study of executive leaders, it was determined that they were remarkably inept at estimating how long tasks required, how to prioritize what was most important, and how truly proficient they were in basic time management. It is no wonder they were constantly frustrated and complained the seminars, workshops, training materials, and apps were pretty worthless in the long run.

I remember one executive I was seeing as a client who was consistently late to almost every session. I confronted her that she didn't seem to make therapy much of a priority and didn't seem to value our time very much. She would apologize profusely and promise to improve the next time, which never happened. She seemed genuinely at a loss to explain this behavior. "I really love these sessions," she'd tell me repeatedly. "They are helping so much! And I do value your time and hate that I'm always late. I don't know what else to do."

"Okay," I replied gently and forgivingly, and I really did believe that her intentions were honorable. But there was something that was clearly getting in her way.

"Let's try an experiment," I suggested.

Feeling so regretful and ashamed, she readily agreed to anything I wanted.

"Let me ask you first: How long do you think it would take you to walk to the drinking fountain down the hall, get a drink of water, and return here? Make as accurate a prediction as you can."

"Hmm, I don't know. Maybe, like, 4 minutes?"

"Is that your best guess?"

"Um, yeah, I'd say four, no, make it 5 minutes." Knowing what I had in mind, she wanted to make certain to pass the test.

She returned 8 minutes later, apologizing once again for being late.

"Interesting, isn't it, how your time estimate was so off?"

She shrugged.

"Okay, then, final experiment. How long do you think it will take you to walk out of the building and get into your car?"

She thought for a few moments, then said cautiously, "Well, I think it will take about 5 or 6 minutes, but maybe I should give myself more time. How about 9 minutes?"

Once again she was off by a lot, not taking into consideration the wait for an elevator, holding the front door open for an elderly person, and stopping at the entrance to respond quickly to a text. It took her almost double her estimate, almost 16 minutes!

During the next session I diagnosed her problem as having a perceptual "disability" with respect to estimating time durations. She admitted that she was almost always late for everything, always missing deadlines, always keeping people waiting in meetings or for appointments. I was hardly the only one who commented on her constant lateness. We fixed the problem by asking her to estimate how long it would take her to get to our next appointment, and then to double it. She was never late again, at least for our sessions.

Self-Care Industries

There is a dark side to self-care, funded and promoted by corporate interests that couldn't care less about the health and well-being of employees, and instead are only concerned with increasing productivity and reducing healthcare costs (Purser, 2019). Companies may set up mindfulness or meditation centers, or other self-care programs alleged to improve morale, yet their effectiveness is measured primarily in terms of expenses reduced from the bottom line. It is just one more example of how self-care is packaged, marketed, and sold as one size fits all rather than truly digging deeply into what might work best for a given individual considering unique interests, preferences, needs, time constraints, capabilities, and personal realities.

Perhaps the most startling example of self-care efforts that mostly fail (except as placebos) is the $2 billion dietary supplement industry that markets itself as the anecdote to aging. Supposedly, ingesting such substances will extend life, stop aging altogether, as well as to provide a host of other benefits, none of which have ever been supported by legitimate evidence. If anything, there is considerable research indicating that some such practices actually increase the risk of diseases and death (Schneider, 2019a; Scudellari, 2015). The FDA provides little oversight over these substances. There are no reliable measures of consistent potency and dosage. There may indeed be some benefit to these supplements but, if so, it has yet to be discovered.

One social worker, inspired to find the best possible self-care program, read all the usual manuals, like "Five Steps to Wellness" or "Seven Must-Have Self-Care Tips," and decided that afterward she felt even worse (Krause, 2017). She asked herself why something that seemed so simple could turn out to be so challenging. Through this exploration she was able to distinguish between the "feel good self-care" that is usually prescribed—having meals delivered, getting a massage, drinking more water—and "sucky self-care" that is really, really tough to do because most of the time you just don't feel like doing it.

Simple self-care is indeed simple and easy because it leads to immediate gratification and rewards. Hugs, chocolate, and back massages feel good right away. Unfortunately, they don't really take care of the reasons why there has been such an erosion of spirit. And when the problem is defined in superficial ways, such as just reducing the number of client contact hours, this may be well intended but doesn't ultimately make much of a difference, except in the industries that increase their profits (Rupert et al., 2015).

Why Self-Care Often Falls Short

We might begin exploring this question by first examining why any effort ultimately fails, starting with therapy itself. In previous projects, a colleague and I (Kottler & Carlson, 2002, 2006, 2011) interviewed dozens of the most prominent theoreticians who were alive at the time to ask them to talk about their most dramatic treatment failures. We never realized how many different ways that negative outcomes could be defined in such different ways. Some theorists refused to even acknowledge that they ever failed, believing instead that the result ultimately "belongs" to the client, not them. Others fully accepted responsibility for treatment disappointments, attributing the lack of success to a host of factors—losing control, a weak relational alliance, making the same mistakes repeatedly, not having a solid plan, being unprepared, or being overconfident.

Among those who tended to disown or deny failure, they offered a number of explanations.

- **Define failure as success.** Although it's clear that your client is not improving significantly, you try to convince him or her, and yourself, that things are really going far better than they really are.
- **Pretend as though you have everything under control.** You feel lost and confused. The truth is that you don't understand what's going on and you don't have a clear idea about where to go next. Nevertheless, you act as though you are well in charge of matters.
- **Blame factors outside of your control.** It can't be your fault that therapy isn't working well. It must have something to do with either the client withholding something, the client's family sabotaging treatment, the "system" undermining your efforts, or bad breaks.

Any of us might offer some of the same kinds of reasons (excuses) for why efforts to take better care of ourselves don't work out very well. They are much the same as the kinds of things our clients tell us all the time, beginning with the hidden benefits and payoffs that accompany such failures. Some people just enjoy a martyr mentality, feeling like they are carrying the burdens of the world as a way to legitimize and justify their own suffering. They earn a kind of grudging respect and admiration, or at least indulgence, from others. They are just far too busy to take care of other undesirable chores around the office or home. They are too exhausted to take care of other business. They're sorry that they lashed out in anger or frustration, but please understand the pressure they are under.

Another benefit is the relief that comes with disowning responsibility and blaming others for the misery. "I just wish I had the time to relax a little, or give myself a break, but there are just too many others who depend on me." That is exactly the reasons most often offered by the cohort of psychiatry residents that

I was supervising during the coronavirus. They had been involuntarily assigned to emergency medicine during the crisis, and as a result were sleep deprived, frightened, overwhelmed, and extremely anxious about the risks they were taking and the fears associated with practicing outside their specialty. And yet with all these pressures many of them were even more neglectful taking care of themselves. When they were offered a support group to help them cope with the stressors the majority indicated they really had little interest, essentially admitting that intimate engagement, mutual support, and self-care were simply not on their radar.

Self-care may not work very well for many of the same reasons our clients fail to stick with their declarations, in spite of their best intentions. Each of us functions within a system that may not necessarily have our own best interests at heart when compared to some other priorities related to profits, public image, political agendas, number crunching, or inflating the power of a few individuals. Without much institutional support we are left to our own devices to try and manage workload and morale. Inevitably there are setbacks and relapses, especially when we must operate within the same unhealthy, stress-infused system.

As part of our jobs, we are frequent witnesses to those conditions and factors that most contribute to enduring changes in people's lives, especially the kinds of adjustments and alterations in self-identity that lead to relatively permanent habit formations. Even after a lifetime of behaving or thinking in particular ways, we have seen, time and time again, how our clients are perfectly capable of making dramatic commitments to their well-being that are consistently maintained. We are also quite familiar with exactly what most likely makes this possible, whether inside therapy or in daily life. The following conditions or characteristics are typical sustaining forces:

> **Dissatisfaction with one's current life predicament.** A condition that leads to uncomfortable symptoms of depression, anxiety, stress, or unhappiness that won't go away unless some significant adjustment is made in one's choices, decisions, and actions.
>
> **Trauma.** Primary trauma, secondary trauma, vicarious trauma, *any* traumatic experience representing extreme disruption of one's life, often leads to significant changes out of desperation.
>
> **Life transitions.** Developmental changes, age-related crises and transitions, similarly require necessary adjustments.
>
> **External events that are beyond one's control.** Natural disasters, economic uncertainty, budget cuts, weather, pandemics, social movements, political instability are all examples of things that often require major changes, no matter how reluctant or avoidant someone might be.

Hitting bottom. The typical scenario with extreme addictions to drugs, alcohol, gambling, shopping, and other such behavior is that the person has to hit bottom in order to finally take charge. In desperation, it feels like everything is lost and there's nothing left to lose. Therapists, as well, sometimes reach this point in which major self-care efforts begin only after it feels like there's no other choice.

Travel. Journeys and adventures, whether literal or metaphorical, often require one to make significant adjustments in novel environments and develop new resources to meet one's needs.

Risk taking. Any attempt to try new behaviors, experiment with new ways of being, face one's fears and challenges, will usually result in increased self-awareness, insight, or commitment.

Lifestyle. Perhaps more important than any other factor related to the potential success of self-care efforts are the choices we make about the ways we structure our lives related to sleep, diet, exercise, social engagements, material consumption, finances, technology, and social support.

What It Takes for Self-Care Strategies to Last

One of the most consistent mistakes that people make when initiating changes in their lives is overreaching—they attempt goals that are far beyond what is realistic and practical, dooming themselves to disappointment and failure. This is not an argument for only declaring modest goals but a recognition that sometimes it is the smallest adjustments that can lead eventually to the most dramatic, sustained efforts. *Keystone behaviors* are little, seemingly insignificant gestures that lead to big changes. With regard to habit formation, Duhigg (2012) cited several examples of this phenomenon in which families that eat dinner together tend to see improvements in children's grades in school, an increase in their self-confidence and well-being, plus greater intimacy and meaningful engagement. Another interesting and peculiar association relates to people who make their beds in the morning and the likelihood of staying on a budget and feeling good about their day as it begins.

There are certain predictors of what is most likely to work as a keystone action that could blossom and grow over time. First of all, it's important to start small and modest, with a behavior that is relatively simple and easy to complete—no matter what. This will likely seem like a ridiculously insignificant gesture, perhaps deciding to start taking the stairs rather than the elevator whenever possible, or making a point to deliberately leave some item of food on your plate.

Although these tiny actions may appear at first to be a drop in the bucket compared to the watershed of relief most people may want and deserve, it is a start. In order to continue the momentum, it's next important to look for ripple effects: What do you notice feels different? What are some things that have changed, in some small way, after sticking with this keystone behavior? The point is that it sometimes takes a series of little, incremental steps before an ultimate goal is reached.

We live and work within organizational systems, each with its own culture and structure, as well as pressures and norms. There is nothing more potentially motivational than public accountability. When you declare to others what you are doing, or intend to do, you are more likely to follow through with commitments. Even better than telling others what you are attempting with a new self-care effort is to recruit them to join you. It isn't a matter of the more the merrier, but rather choosing wisely and selectively partners you can trust to be reliable, conscientious, and committed to the actions over time, those you can depend on to keep you on course.

We are also more enlightened than most others about what makes changes last besides public commitments and social support. It helps to be scrupulously honest and transparent about what is possible and realistic, committing to the sort of ongoing critical self-monitoring that accompanies systematic assessment over time as to what is working and what is not.

One of the scenarios we see most often are clients who engage in obviously self-defeating behavior that clearly doesn't work, yet they insist on continuing these actions in the face of overwhelming evidence of their ineffectiveness. Since it is our passion, excitement, and enthusiasm that help immunize us against the stressors that arise, boredom and complacency can become our worst enemies. It is really difficult to see dozens of clients each week, year after year, hearing variations of the same stories every day, if not each session, and not feel weary by the predictable nature of the work. We each have within our repertoire a series of favorite techniques, seminal stories we like to tell, standard interventions, automatic responses, that become well-worn over time. It takes considerable commitment and persistence to recognize these signs and symptoms of complacency, since the awareness means we have to get back to work and do things differently. We are sometimes just as resistant to doing so as any of our clients, particularly when we are already pretty familiar and uncomfortable with the status quo.

All day long we help others to reinvent themselves, to take on a different identity that is far more self-enhancing, or at least to escape settling for mediocrity. Although I've known plenty of excellent therapists who have been practicing their same craft the same way for years, if not decades, without significantly changing their style, I've also known many others who have chosen a different pathway to continued professional viability by continuously upgrading, changing, even completely transforming the ways they work. As we are exposed to new research, novel treatment models, updates and developments in therapeutic practice, we adapt our methods. Perhaps even more impactful are the ways our clients become our greatest teachers, challenging us to make major adjustments, loosening the bonds of our own rigidity, sending clear messages that what we have been doing previously is not something they wish to continue. We are encouraged to experiment with new ways of being, to become far more creative in the ways we conceptualize our work. Ultimately, if we continue to reinvent ourselves over time, we are rewarded with the most satisfying achievement of all—that we have developed a therapeutic style that truly best features our signature strengths and our own unique voice. That is never a static condition but rather one that is continually evolving in light of new experiences, both as part of professional training as well as in our personal lives.

Organizational Dysfunctions and Toxic Cultures

When helping professionals are asked what they find most stressful and unnerving about their work, they often mention things like the following:

> "I have expenses to pay and debts to pay off but I don't get enough referrals from my agency to count on enough sessions each week. They promised me enough work to do but they tell everyone that same thing and we have to compete with one another."

> "There's this one guy in the office who is so incredibly rude and insensitive. He bullies others and plays games with all of us but nobody will do or say anything because he's friends with the director."

> "I come in each day and look at my schedule and there are times I just shake my head. What are they thinking that we can possibly handle so many difficult cases in a day, with so little time to catch our breath and take care of all their stupid paper work."

> "Truthfully, my supervisor has no clue what's going on. I don't even know how this person got this job but now I'm stuck trying to pretend that this arrangement is suitable."

> "I have to share an office with two other people and we are always fighting for space. I don't know how they expect us to do our jobs when we don't even have much privacy."

> "They tell us that we have to abide by these stupid rules and regulations that the board developed, but none of these people have actually done any clinical work in decades. They don't seem to understand what we are dealing with."

> "We are divided into treatment teams supposedly to encourage collaboration but what actually happens is that we try to undermine one another since there are limited resources and our grant money is being cut back."

"The systems in place that are designed to protect us from excessive workload and pressure stopped working years ago but nobody seems to care. It's like we are working in a factory and all they care about is that the assembly line moves people in and out as fast as possible."

Among all the examples about the kinds of systemic dysfunctions within mental health agencies that contribute to stress, the most extreme was the story shared by a psychiatric nurse working in an inpatient unit. She was assigned a case of a man who reported that he had dozens of poisonous snakes crawling around in his belly. She was required to discharge this patient when they managed to reduce the number of poisonous snakes to just three, supposedly demonstrating a successful outcome.

It is virtually impossible to understand and address the stress, burnout, and life dissatisfaction of anyone without considering the context of their experience within their lives and particular job. When a professional or employee is dissatisfied, disgruntled, frustrated, or overwhelmed it is not just because of their own thinking, behavior, and self-care neglect, but also results from forces within the work setting (Dimitrios & Konstantinos, 2014; Mavridis et al., 2019).

Figley (1995, 2002) was among the first to discuss the cultural and organizational context for burnout and compromised self-care as part of several characteristics of this syndrome. There was, of course, the cognitive domain in which particular kinds of thinking (perfectionism, rigidity, distractibility, apathy) lead to discouragement. Likewise, on an emotional level, those who exhibit fear, anger, guilt, shame, anxiety, and depression are bound to encounter difficulties in their work. Then there are behavioral indices related to impatience, social withdrawal, neglect, and fatigue, just as there is a perceived lack of meaning in the mission. But one of the most influential factors of all relates to interpersonal relationships in the context of the work climate. This is described as the collective perception of team members regarding their characteristics, goals, values, and job demands (Kozusznik et al., 2015). This environmental/social climate may be classified in the same way as any individual's response to challenges—distressed, eustressed, or balanced.

There are particular social norms, organizational climates, assigned roles, and job demands that virtually guarantee that people will struggle mightily. When colleagues undermine and sabotage one another, engage in disruptive conflict, or demonstrate a lack of respect and trust toward others, there is going to be collateral damage. When oversight and supervision are marginal or laissez faire, when bullies are allowed to run over others, when there are perceived inequities and unjust practices, when there is overt or disguised racism, sexism, ageism, homophobia, when the workload is unreasonable, when resources are sorely limited, when ... Well, certainly you can add to this list of all the forces and features of a job that lead to discouragement (see Table 6.1).

Table 6.1 TOXIC INFLUENCES WITHIN ORGANIZATIONAL CULTURES

Lack of coherent vision and consistent mission	Gossip and undermining
Leader instability and incompetence	Contagious complaining and whining
Leader micromanagement and overcontrol	High turnover among staff
Bureaucratic rules and regulations that stifle initiative	Competitive and conflicted relationships
Budget cuts and limited resources	Atmosphere of uncertainty and fear
Excessive impromptu meetings	Minimal support and encouragement among staff
Unexpected crises and ongoing chaos	No follow through on commitments
Excessive workload	Isolation and disengagement from community
Abusive, unappreciative clients	Excessive tracking, paperwork, and data collection

I have quit so many jobs in my life because of toxic cultures with so many of the features mentioned in Table 6.1. During my first clinical placement with adolescents, my supervisor used to listen to our conversations through the walls and then tap loudly when she disagreed with something I was saying or doing. This would require my clients and I to whisper conspiratorially so she couldn't interrupt us (which actually led to faster trust and intimacy). In my first academic job, there was only one other colleague in our small graduate program. She was a very nice woman but she believed that the best and only way to help people was to pray together with them. I've had other jobs that were exercises in complete chaos; still others were so regimented and controlled we had to ask permission to do almost anything. But by far the worst, most stressful, soul-destroying job ever was in a large academic department with a department head who had a diagnosable explosive personality disorder. He would scream at people, lapse into fits of rage, become so abusive at times that many would run away sobbing. And yet, typical of such a dynamic, his behavior would not have been permitted to continue if everyone else did not somehow enable his behavior and fail to challenge it. I've fled all those jobs and so many others, each of which presented an environment that made it difficult, if not impossible, to function very well.

Since those days I've spent a lot of time interviewing therapists, counselors, teachers, nurses, physicians, corporate leaders, and other helping professionals about what most leads to stress, burnout, and difficulties in their work. Interestingly, they rarely mention the demands of their clients, patients, or customers, no matter how challenging the cases or intractable their problems. Instead they frequently mention either their supervisor's incompetence or neglect, or else the lack of support they get from their coworkers.

It has been suggested that one of the single best ways to maintain a culture of self-care at work is by building or creating a "greenhouse" the encourages and sustains healthy growth and support (Skovholt & Trotter-Mathison, 2016). For reasons I've never understood, or been able to explain, mental health professionals have a reputation of being pretty uncivil to one another at times. One reason is that our field sometimes attracts more than its fair share of narcissistic people who enjoy dominating others. After all, what better training exists to exploit, control, and manipulate people? Also, as we are certainly aware, all it takes is for one toxic colleague to be tolerated, if not enabled, in order to pollute a culture of goodwill and cooperation. I've heard more than a few therapists complain that the most challenging aspect of their jobs isn't dealing with difficult clients but rather their own frustrating and abusive peers.

If the main reason that professionals in any field hate their jobs, or find them inordinately stressful, is because their supervisor doesn't know what the hell he or she is doing, or else is not supportive (or is even abusive), then it makes sense that this would apply to us as well. Most of us have had the experience of being micromanaged, or neglected, by someone who is supposed to have our best interests at heart but only seems to care about self-promotion and maintaining power. On the other hand, laissez faire leaders may readily witness a lack of caring and support in the workplace but do absolutely nothing to address these dysfunctions, allowing resentments and conflicts to fester.

In summary, most self-care efforts that are not sustained are often undermined not by a lack of desire or intention but rather by the systems and culture in which we function. When we don't feel sufficient support and encouragement from colleagues and supervisors it is inevitable that eventually increased stress and burnout will result. Likewise, if we do not have nurturing friends and family members as an integral part of our lives, we don't have the opportunity to fully process and metabolize the disturbing, overwhelming interactions we experience as part of our daily jobs. Any strategies that we incorporate into our habits and routines must take into consideration the larger social, interpersonal, political, and economic forces at work.

CHAPTER 7

Strategies That Probably (or Might) Make a Difference

This is probably not the most inspirational, encouraging title for a chapter, is it? But I'm trying to be honest. After all, you already know what to do to reduce stress and improve the quality of life, with your own clients as well as yourself. You've heard the same things over and over, if not offered the same advice to others: Stop checking your phone every few minutes. Get out of the chair and stretch, or walk a little. Drink more water. Take some deep, cleansing breaths.

But of course you are too busy. Or you get distracted. Or you don't have time. Or you forget. Or you don't have that much control over your time and schedule. Or ... Let's just agree that reading books like this, or attending workshops and seminars on the subject, are responses to a desperate need for encouragement; however, the effects rarely last very long once we are fully immersed back in the chaos of our lives.

It is interesting, if not exactly surprising, that helping professionals experience and report their self-care strategies in as many different ways as they describe their symptoms of stress and difficulty. We operate in so many different ways, depending on work setting, client population, previous history, preferred theoretical orientation, personality, agency policies and regulations, cultural climate, and so many other factors. What is both universal and clear, however, is that almost all practitioners struggle with taking better care of themselves and attempt to do so mostly on their own without much help from their organization, supervisors, or even colleagues (Sawicki, 2019).

Just as I was writing the passage above, I received a "bing," signaling a text from a colleague who I had written earlier in the day. He had asked me how I was doing and I poured my heart out to him, sharing that my father died a few weeks ago, my best friend was just diagnosed with terminal cancer, I was experiencing some health issues, plus I was struggling to redefine my professional identity and where I was headed next in my career. In addition,

I mentioned that I was troubled about a new commitment I'd agreed to that I didn't think I was qualified and adequately prepared to handle. When I heard the signal that his response came in I felt immediate relief that support and counsel had finally arrived. What I found instead was a single, solitary emoji, a ♥ indicating that apparently he "liked" what I said. That's the kind of encouragement we've come to expect these days. People wear ribbons to show their support for a cause. They click on a post to demonstrate their favoritism toward a comment. This so-called "slacktivism" saves time and energy and we've now become accustomed to such superficial levels of caring.

These quick, easy, and convenient responses to life's issues and problems are also related to self-care strategies. We discussed previously how people are overreliant on simplistic cures, books, apps, programs, and tools that are alleged to offer instant cures for stress, time management, weight loss, addictions, or anything else, but they are predicated on an existing skill set to put them into practice. These are the kinds of behaviors that require long, hard work to learn and internalize. These "life hacks" don't work well for reasons already mentioned, most notably that most people are not good at accurately and honestly assessing how long tasks take or at predicting what unforeseen things might end up on their schedule Dierdorff (2020) instead found that it wasn't the particular self-care program or strategy that mattered very much as compared to developing several basic skills related to managing one's time better:

1. **Study, assess, and determine the best part of the day to get things done.** Whether that is the morning, afternoon, or evening, or particular days of the week, it's important to find peak performance times, as well as the least productive times because of flagging energy, distractions, or multiple demands.

2. **Realistically evaluate your predictive ability to estimate task completion.** A planned schedule is only useful if it represents a clear and accurate representation of what actually occurs. If you are consistently underestimating the difficulty and length of tasks and projects, then it's time to make needed adjustments.

3. **Charge yourself an hourly rate.** Figure out what your hourly rate is for professional services. Whether that is $50 or $500 per hour, treat your discretionary and personal time as if it is just as valuable a commodity as what you "sell" to others. After all, why should your time priorities and scheduling be so critical when it comes to helping others but taken for granted when not on the clock? I remember once shopping for a shirt at a department store and the salesperson told me if I returned the following day I could save 40%, which seemed like a good deal. But then I calculated

what it would cost me in terms of the amount of time to drive over again, park, find a space, wait for a cashier, assuming I could find the shirt again, and it struck me that I'd be paying triple for that shirt if I considered what my time was worth. Ever since that day I've asked myself how much my time is worth whenever I'm considering an action.

4. **Prioritize what is most important.** Determine what things you spend too much time doing that don't matter in any significant way. They don't result in outcomes that appreciably increase your job and life satisfaction, or even seem very efficient. People often spend way too much time doing things that just "waste" time in the sense that they provide neither much pleasure nor satisfaction. If watching a "stupid" program, or playing a "dumb" game, helps you to chill out and turn your brain off, that can actually be worthwhile. But I'm referring more to the time-squandering things that do absolutely nothing except leave you further behind in the stuff you stay is most important. Of course these activities could also represent avoidance strategies, in which case it's time to examine those more critically as well.

5. **Determine cost–benefit outcomes.** If you are spending too much time on a task, activity, project, or case that doesn't seem to result in significant benefits considering the investment, then maybe it's better to move on to something more profitable. As I get older, and the aging clock is winding down, I've become more and more discerning about how I'm willing to spend my time on things that don't seem to matter very much at all. It's not just about calculating whether the compensation is worth the energy—which doesn't matter as much to me now considering so many of the things I do are pro bono—but rather whether this is actually the most advantageous, potent way that I could spend my time as opposed to doing something else.

These are just a few examples of the kinds of skills that are actually needed in order to make any self-care strategy actually make much of a difference.

Sitting Still All Day

What therapists and other helping professionals do for a living is sit very, very still in a chair and listen to other people talk. This work environment is quite at odds with the ways that evolution designed our bodies. Among all the creatures on the planet human beings were built as distance athletes, running 20 miles each day to hunt and gather food. Nowadays we barely shuffle from one chair or couch to another, spending the majority of the hours relatively immobile. For therapists and many other health professionals our time is occupied in perfect stillness much of the day, sitting in a chair, listening to people talk to us.

We are not permitted to get up and walk around, or even fidget, or else we might be viewed as restless, if not bored (which we are some of the time). We are mostly confined to a room, a private, soundproofed vault, insulated from the rest of the world and free of all distractions and intrusions. Clients rotate in and out of our offices all day long, just as we remain immobile statues, burning calories by nodding our heads. There's little doubt that such an inactive lifestyle increases the risk of health problems and makes self-care even more challenging.

Let's begin with the basics, the same sort of things we tell our clients. The most important features of any self-care program involve keeping our bodies in optimal condition; everything else flows from that. We've all heard—and recommended—the usual suspects: (a) a nutritional, healthy diet; (b) regular exercise and movement; (c) sufficient sleep; (d) periodic rest and recovery time; and (e) supportive relationships and social engagement. You can conduct your own inventory of how well you are managing these aspects of your daily routine; problems persist when a few of them are being neglected.

The vast majority of professionals report that they exercise on a regular basis. But then again self-reports are often unreliable for the same reason that people sign up for classes, trainers, coaches, or fitness clubs or programs, but rarely use the services. The reality is that the vast majority of Americans (80%!) walk less than one third of a mile a day—and that includes strolling around the house or getting up from the chair to grab a cup of coffee. By the way, the same percentage of people who refuse to walk more than a few hundred steps each day corresponds to the number of people who are considered significantly overweight.

It's also interesting that although a regular exercise routine has been consistently found as one of the best means to reduce stress and burnout at work, it doesn't necessarily lead to increased productivity unless other steps are also taken (Pope, 2017; Weir, 2011). A pretty compelling and humorous example of this relates to corporations trying to bribe and incentivize their employees to become more physically active by asking them to wear activity trackers to count their steps in order to obtain some reward. But alas, some people have simply attached the trackers to their dogs in order to raise their scores without having to pry themselves out of their chairs (Bartleby, 2019).

There is likely no other self-care habit that is more beneficial, healthy, empowering, and soothing (however much commitment, work, and suffering is involved) than physical exercise. This had been suspected for some time but it wasn't until after World War II that a budget-strapped medical researcher settled on an efficient and brilliant way to empirically test the idea. Jeremy Morris had noticed that the characteristic double decker buses in London might be the perfect laboratory to test his theory. He had noticed that the two employees of each bus had very different jobs. The driver sat in his seat all day, relatively immobile and comfortable, while the conductor climbed up and down steps all day long checking tickets, 600 steps every shift. It was, therefore, a relatively straightforward matter to track the health and longevity of the bus workers—over 30,000 of them over time. Morris was able to compare the two groups and discovered that the drivers were twice as likely to die of a heart attack, after controlling and adjusting for other health factors. Bryson (2019) mentions this story as one of the first systematic studies to demonstrate, consistently and overwhelmingly, that exercise—even just going for a walk for a few minutes each day—significantly increased life expectancy and improved well-being. And this is in addition to all the physical benefits of strengthening bones and improving the functioning of every system in the body. "If someone invented a pill that could do for us all that a moderate amount of exercise achieves," he summarized, "it would instantly become the most successful drug in history" (p. 179).

It turns out that there is nothing special about the magical 10,000 steps that are often recommended on apps, or the Center for Disease Control's prescription of 150 minutes per week. *Anything* we do to increase active mobility, however limited, still makes a difference. And it is precisely because it is challenging to do on a regular basis, and stick with the commitment, that it adds to the benefit of increasing self-discipline and a sense of daily achievement, no matter what else we are dealing with. Considering that gluttony and obesity are currently among the greatest health risks, exercise also helps in that domain.

In summary, if there is one single habit that best immunizes people against stress and anxieties, the answer is definitive: consistent, daily physical exercise. Immunologists, endocrinologists, and neurologists have found that exercise best simulates the same internal responses that occur during stress, thus buffering the effects of all the hormonal circulation that can become toxic (Joshu, 2019a; Wunsch et al., 2019). Whether running, aerobic classes, fast walking, or any other activity that is internalized as a habit, these activities help to accommodate our systems to arousal in healthy ways because they produce similar physiological reactions to what occurs when we feel overwhelmed by life events—elevated respiration and cardiac activity, sweating, boosts of the endocrine system for energy. They condition us to metabolize high-intensity resistance training. However (and this is a big "however"), like everything else related to self-care activities, the benefits depend on the ways that people think about their habits (Ciccolo, 2019). For those who associate exercise with inconvenience, suffering, and annoyance, there are minimal effects compared to those who have taught themselves to embrace these choices as invigorating and stimulating.

Obsessions With Mindfulness

Practicing mindfulness is often purported to be the do-all, end-all panacea for anything that bothers us. Engage in breathing exercises, curate the mind to focus on a mantra or mandala, do some yoga postures or Tai Chi, or simply concentrate and give purposeful attention to the present moment—and voila!—instant relief. There is certainly considerable evidence to support the value of such mindful habits to reduce stress, decrease disturbing thoughts, improve emotional control, and restore a sense of stability—and all that is quite encouraging. Unfortunately, like many other popular self-care methods, it is not nearly enough when there are other systemic forces at work that return you to the same conflicted arena once your incantations, prayers, or silent meditation is completed. It is also interesting, and a little ironic, that although a number of self-care benefits are consistently reported, there is little indication that this actually makes us better at our jobs or produces better outcomes (Norcross & VandenBos, 2018).

What is undeniable is that those who practice mindfulness, whether periods of silent reflection, meditation, stillness, visualization, progressive relaxation, journaling, stretching, self-compassion exercises, or yoga, on a regular basis, do enjoy a number of self-care advantages (Davis & Hayes, 2012; Geller, 2017), although the benefits depend, on the professional's personality, particular challenges, and cultural norms of the job (Krick & Felfe, 2019). Nevertheless, there are often distinct outcomes reported:

- reduced stress and anxiety
- heightened awareness of sensations and experiences
- increased memory, concentration, and focus
- diminished rumination and negative cognition
- recovery from trauma
- reduced perception of pain and suffering
- new insights and reflective awareness
- improved sense of well-being
- increased empathy and compassion for others

Mindfulness had emerged as the fifth (or maybe sixth or seventh these days) therapeutic wave in recent years, the latest craze to fix whatever is wrong. There is mindfulness-based stress reduction therapy, mindfulness-based cognitive therapy, dialectical behavior therapy, mindfulness-awareness practice, acceptance and commitment therapy, mindfulness meditation, creative visualization, mindful breathing techniques, to mention a few of the popular options on the scene. What they all have in common is a focus on greater awareness of inner sensations, thoughts, and feelings accompanied with the skills to alter this internal landscape through breathing, stretching, visualizing, or thinking techniques.

The reality is that nowadays almost every therapeutic approach makes use of these methods in some variation. Behavior therapy was always associated with relaxation methods as part of systematic desensitization for stress, phobias, and fears. Every cognitive therapy makes use of self-talk in some way to alter dysfunctional patterns. All the brief, problem-solving therapies utilize forms of reframing or redefining the problem in a way that makes it more amenable to change, thus altering our perception and relationship with the issue. They are also inclined to use breathing, hypnotic inductions, and imagery as a means by which to imagine a different future or unique outcome.

Regardless of theoretical allegiances, we may frequently ask our clients what they are telling themselves about their predicaments—and how they might think about the situation differently in more forgiving or functional ways. We are vulnerable to similar kinds of perseverating about stressors in our lives. There are endless ruminations about things we said that we wish we hadn't, or things we've done that we regret, or things we didn't say that we are now rehearsing endlessly with incessant ruminations.

"Ground zero for creating a healthy work-life balance is not in the real world," Winch (2019) reminds us. "It's in our head. It's with ruminating. If you want to reduce your stress and improve your quality of life, you don't necessarily have to change your hours or your job. You just have to change how you think."

This of course sounds very familiar since it is what we tell others all the time, even if we sometimes forget to internalize the message ourselves when we feel overwhelmed. Winch makes the point that we actually don't experience as much stress *during* work as we do after we are home and trying so hard to recover from it. *That* is when we begin ruminating about our mistakes and lapses, feeling the crushing burden of how we can possibly catch up to all that we have to do when we complain over and over, "I have so much to do!" The mind-altering response to that, as Winch suggests, is reformulating the declaration into problem statements that can be solved:

- "How can I make adjustments in my schedule to give myself more breaks?"
- "What spaces can I create within the day that would reduce the burdens I feel?"
- "What am I willing to let go of in order to reduce the pressure?"
- "What support might be available to assist me with everything on my agenda?"
- "What are some ways I might think differently about what is happening?"

This is hardly a novel or unusual suggestion, since these sorts of questions are exactly the kinds of things we talk about all day long with those who beseech us for relief from their misery. But once again revisiting the main theme of the book: We are sometimes hypocrites for not practicing in our lives what we urge others to do.

Keeping a Stress Journal

This is another resource that we often recommend to our clients—keeping a record of their innermost thoughts and feelings that are most disturbing, as well as talking through a constructive process of countering negative feelings and unrealistic thinking. When focused on the theme of stress, we are able to accumulate a consistent, accurate document that highlights exactly when, how, and why we are most often triggered, as well as what seems to help the most to calm us down. It's pretty interesting to try this out for a single day as an experiment, just to note when you feel most anxious or upset about something. Here are a few examples from a single day in my life:

Day/Time	Place	Context	What Happened?	Reactions	Thoughts
Monday, 11:10 AM	Office	Waiting for client who cancelled with little notice last week	Client never showed up and didn't call	Frustration, anger, feeling abused and unappreciated	I knew this would happen!
Monday, 1:40 PM	Office	Toward the end of what seems like a productive, helpful session	Client complained therapy isn't help-ing and wants to quit	Confusion, uncertainty, frustration	This seems to be happening more and more often. Am I losing my magic?
Monday, 6:10 PM	Running to car	Running late for meeting because ses-sion ran over time and case files had to be completed	Overscheduled myself with too much to do within time available	Extremely anxious since I hate to run late; disap-pointed in myself again	My life feels out of control at times, directed by forces beyond me

We urge our clients to slow down the pace of their lives, providing time to reflect on the viability of their choices and meaning of their actions. Likewise, our own lives are filled with stress because we are always rushing everywhere, behind schedule to finish tasks, and trying to do too many things at the same time. It is not unusual to find yourself having a conversation with someone on the phone while you are checking email, glancing at a magazine, and nibbling on a snack.

Back to the value of mindfulness again to remind us to slow down our lives in order to just to do one thing at a time, as deliberately, intentionally, and consciously as possible. Whether munching on a snack, walking to the bathroom, staring out the window, the goal is to focus all attention and energy on doing that one thing as mindfully as possible. Begin by sitting quietly for a few minutes and do absolutely *nothing* else except that activity.

These sorts of self-monitoring tools for daily stress are now the rage, part of the billion-dollar self-care empire that aims to cure whatever bothers you. Therapists are now being replaced, or at least augmented, by mobile software apps that promise relief from daily pressures. These include Headspace (breathing exercises), Anxietycoach (CBT for fears), Moodtools (thought diary), Calm (meditation), and Happify (soothing activities), all of which claim they are far better than merely keeping a written record since these are supposedly "evidence-based." As to what kind of "evidence" supports their claims, it is mostly reports from a few satisfied customers who managed to stick with them for more than a few weeks.

Of course any tool, device, program, or app that keeps one consistently dedicated to better self-care is useful, but only if it leads to habituation that eventually becomes internalized.

Things That You Can Do Every Day

During my earliest years in school I remember a teacher introducing us to the new, popular curriculum of values clarification exercises. The idea was to help teenagers during their identity formative years to explore and solidify values, attitudes, and activities that defined who we were and provided the most satisfaction and joy. We were asked to make a list of more than a dozen such "Things We Love to Do." There are a number of variations related to this exercise, in which we might be asked to rank order the items according to how important they are, or to note if they cost more or less than $5, or whether we were inclined to do them alone, or with someone else, but the main point was to declare the things that gave us the most pleasure and then to note how often we do them and when the last time was that we engaged in this activity. It's been more than a half century since I first did this exercise and I'm not that surprised that the first items on my list—sex, skiing, and intimate conversations—are still among my highest priorities (even if their order has changed).

The point of this exercise was not only to commit to what matters most to us on a daily basis, but to put it in writing so we are held accountable for what we say is most important. If these are precisely the things that give us most satisfaction, why aren't we making a point to do them more regularly?

If you consider what you love to do the most that reduces your stress, improves your mood, and increases your life satisfaction, what would you add to your own list? What are the specific activities that you'd be prepared to do each day, *every* day, in order to create a more active, healthy lifestyle? The particular items on your list could include anything, however small and insignificant, that helps you to feel better about your day—and that feels like you are taking better care of yourself without negative side effects.

Just Take a Break

When helping professionals are asked what they do to take care of themselves during times of unrelenting stress, they most often mention the same things their clients might do—practice mindfulness and meditation (65%), exercise (40%), and so on. But interestingly, when they are asked what could actually help them the most to reduce pressure, enhance work satisfaction, and increase well-being, two-thirds of them mentioned either stepping away for short breaks more often, or else reaching out more proactively for support from coworkers and supervisors (Mavridis et al., 2019).

It would appear, then, that the most important aspects of self-care may not relate at all to our own focused efforts that just add to the burden, but rather to the simplest intentions to take regular breathers as needed, spend simple time alone, and reach out to others for support and nurturance. We operate in such an insulated world much of time, sequestered inside an office, that we sometimes forget to notice when we start feeling out of sorts.

Any of the strategies mentioned in this chapter are potentially helpful only for relatively moderate levels of stress, as opposed to times when we are so overwhelmed and discouraged that very little will put a dent in the burnout that has taken hold (Mavridis et al., 2019). It is crucial, therefore, to recognize the earliest signs and symptoms of stress before they get beyond the point that self-care interventions can help ameliorate the situation.

How do you know when it's time for a break? Of course each of us has different trigger points, but generally we look for the same symptoms we discover in our clients—sleep disruption; appetite (and weight) gain or loss; physical complaints without organic causes; lingering depression and discouragement; dysphoric mood swings; intrusive, negative thoughts; feelings of helplessness; and so on. It is important to detect the earliest signs of trouble before stress becomes too severe, which is an ambitious and sometimes unrealistic goal considering that it is the nature of our human condition to not seek help until we have reached a point of desperation.

I recall three different times in my professional life in which I reached a point of such despair. In each case I had come to dread some aspects of my work, usually not because of my clients/students/supervisees but rather because of disruptive, insensitive behavior on the part of colleagues. Even though several of us complained constantly about the toxic culture and disruptive actions on the part of a few people, this went on for years and years. We would reinforce one another's position as a victim, trade war stories of how badly we were treated, and almost compete with one another about how miserable each of us was. I've noticed similar phenomena with respect to couples divorcing, in which I'd ask the person initiating the breakup how long he or she had known the relationship was over and frequently I'd hear "more than 5 years." In other words, it is rare that anyone notices the first signs and symptoms of dissatisfaction or discomfort and that sparks decisive action; more often we have to reach a state of quiet (or loud) desperation.

We have each learned to become diligent students of our own bodies, recognizing when something is out of balance or some nagging annoyance or discomfort is a sign of some underlying problem. We literally feel it in our bones, or at least our muscles. For most of us, it might be a loss of energy, or perhaps lack of interest in activities that usually give us pleasure. Trouble falling asleep, or frequently awaking, are also clear signs that something is wrong. And perhaps most significant of all is when we start depending on habits (or addictions) to take the edge off the pressure, whether shopping sprees or overdependence on substances, drugs, or alcohol.

Most of the suggestions and strategies mentioned in this chapter, and almost everywhere else, focus on activities, strategies, techniques, things to *do*. Yet some religious leaders contend that the overwhelming stress in life is the result of struggles within the material world of acquisition and achievement, and neglecting spiritual nourishment. The "sabbath antidote" is offered as a radical alternative, one that reclaims almost two months of vacation each year simply by deciding to do absolutely nothing on one day each week (Leder, 2019). Honoring this sabbath means taking one day off to rest, relax, refrain from buying anything or doing any work whatsoever. No shopping, online or at the mall. No texting or social media. Living a seventh of your life with minimal stress to replenish your spirit. This is certainly an admirable goal but also one that is so difficult to achieve in today's all-access, 24-hour-a-day connections.

Some Difficult Conversations

As highlighted above, and throughout earlier discussions, so much of work satisfaction comes not just from helping our clients in a way that feels productive and meaningful, but also getting along with other staff. Sometimes others take advantage of us, engage in unfair or unjust practices, and behave insensitively or incompetently. Administrators are inclined to push for greater productivity regardless of the consequences on staff well-being. Morale is often an afterthought, an intangible variable that is not considered much of a priority.

When consulting with medical professionals and therapists about their frustrations and challenges at work one of the most common themes relates to feeling unsupported and undermined by supervisors, administrators, or colleagues. Under such circumstances there are three viable options. The first is often unrealistic and impractical: quit the job and go somewhere else. The second option is also less than desirable: just keep your head down, accept the way things are, and endure the situation no matter how challenging it might be. The third option, and by far the one that is preferable, is to find a way to change the current dynamics, at least in modest ways that make things more tenable.

There are times when it is useful, even necessary, to sit down with someone and initiate a difficult conversation about the current state of affairs. Maybe this is with a colleague who keeps pushing or annoying you in a way that feels disrespectful. Perhaps it is with a family member, partner, roommate, or friend who doesn't quite understand the nature of your job and the pressure you are under. It could be with an administrator or supervisor who keeps overloading you with more than you can reasonably handle. Sometimes this tough conversation needs to be with yourself, drawing a line in the sand about how much more you can take under the current circumstances.

The single most important self-care strategy of all involves being realistic and scrupulously honest about the burdens you can carry on your shoulders without feeling the crushing pressure that takes its toll. When the demands of a job exceed one's capabilities then it is necessary to set inviolate boundaries and firm limits, no matter what others expect. If those in power and control are unwilling to renegotiate or adjust expectations, then it is time to look for something else to do, or somewhere else to do what you once loved.

Do Something!

As this discussion comes to a close, one can justifiably wonder if it truly matters what you do to take better care of yourself—as long as you do *something*, and do it consistently. If research reveals that each of us views self-care in a unique and personal way, then it also makes sense that one size does not fit all when it comes to effective strategies. Some of us are "built" for vigorous, strenuous exercise, hours of a grueling regimen, while others are better suited for just chilling in a favorite spot and turning the brain off altogether. Whether training and running ultramarathons, practicing Tai Chi or yoga, hanging out with friends, cooking a festive meal, or just exercising greater discipline in setting limits and reducing schedule demands, there is no single option that works best for everyone. Well, I take that back: It *does* appear that regular exercise in some form really is the answer if the goal is to better metabolize stress and improve health. And if the goal is to truly sustain the effort over time, the self-care strategy must have several features.

- **Individualized and personalized focus and goal.** It should represent something you truly enjoy and love, rather than another obligation and burden.
- **Passionate commitment and engagement.** Ideally the choice should feel like a gift to yourself, a treasured opportunity.
- **Resilience and recovery.** Pay attention to the results and relative benefits: Are the time and energy commitments producing the outcomes you desire?

If you were hoping for an endless catalog of foolproof, evidence-supported, empirically tested self-care strategies that right every wrong and restore you to optimal functioning with minimal fuss, then you are likely mighty disappointed. Many people buy or read books like this hoping for the one antidote to stress and path to nirvana that they have yet to consider, especially one that requires minimal effort and is guaranteed to be effective. I seriously wondered if I should skip a chapter like this in the book altogether since, ultimately, the specific strategy doesn't mean very much—and there are literally thousands of other options available on the market. If each of us defines and conceptualizes self-care in a different way (which seems to be the case) then it also makes sense that what would work for one person might not work for others. It really doesn't matter exactly what we do, as long as we do something to take better care of ourselves. Acts of intention matter—but not as much as sustained effort in which you ritualize some behaviors, activities, or strategies into your life. Every single day.

CHAPTER 8

The Nature of Healthy Habits

Habits are deeply ingrained patterns of behavior, meaning they are relatively permanently grooved into neuropathways in the brain. The brain—if it could express its own preferences—absolutely *loves* these automatic responses that free it to focus its mind on other, more important, novel situations that crop up. They save time and energy. In fact, half of all one's choices, decisions, actions, and behavior are not made consciously at all but rather follow patterns long established. From morning rituals of brushing teeth, or putting one shoe on before the other, favorite meal choices, and routes to school, work, or home, evolution provided us with the means to conserve effort and routine thinking processes so that the size of the brain (and head) could be reduced to squeeze out of the birth canal. Without this programmed, automatic behavior we'd become paralyzed when making every little decision regarding which shoe to put on first or even which hand to use for the task.

Habitual behavior occupies such a significant part of our lives that it helps explain why making self-care changes is so incredibly difficult. Almost 90% of daily hygiene tasks, like washing, shaving, and brushing teeth, are controlled by habit. More than half of the things people do at work are routine, habitual activities without much thought. You regularly start and end most sessions or treatments the same way. You sit in the same seat every time. You take care of case notes following previous patterns. The same is true with respect to anything related to rest or relaxation. And even physical activities like working out and playing sports are controlled primarily by habits from rehearsed practice (Wood, 2019).

Although we may prefer to enjoy the illusion that we are active agents in our daily lives, mostly in control of our personal choices and actions, much of the time we are simply robots responding to automatic cues that were established long ago. One example of this is evident in the ways we most commonly behave in a supermarket, automatically navigating the aisles in the same sequence and route that we have followed previously, rarely departing from this established program that makes daily actions so much simpler and effortless.

The Brain Loves Habits

The birth of a habit usually begins with a particular originating thought that leads to some intention or choice, one that is immediately rewarded or reinforced in some way. All this action initially takes place in the basal ganglia, the decision-making areas of the brain. Once these satisfying actions are repeated several times, the brain rewires the neurons to send signals to the sensorimotor region, where more routine behaviors are controlled. If the actions continue to be repeated enough times (usually more than a few dozen) then it is considered a habit that is now elicited by particular contextual and situational cues rather than any deliberate choice or preference.

Just as rats or pigeons have been conditioned to respond in particular ways, each of us has become programmed through a series of sensorimotor loops to reduce the amount of time and energy we must spend thinking about routine actions. What once started out as a choice or decision eventually becomes automatic once it is found to be efficient, useful, or satisfying—at least initially.

Each habit has its own neural signature, indicating that repetitive decisions and choices that are initially made in the cerebral cortex, taking up space in working memory, can instead be shifted from such goal-directed behavior to a context cue response, in which the behavior is triggered in the future by recognizable signals that remain beyond conscious awareness (Wood & Runger, 2016). As long as the established habitual responses are functional and useful, without negative side effects, this remains an extremely efficient way to go about routine business. You don't have to think about whether you are going to work out, or eat dessert, or have coffee; they are automatic responses to environmental, contextual cues.

On the other hand, if and when we engage in so-called "bad" habits—working excessively, relying on mind-altering substances, taking unnecessary risks, gambling, and other addictions—these behaviors are particularly resistant to extinction as long as the triggers and cues in the environment or the mind remain present. Given that these automatic responses take place without explicit consent, or even awareness, that's one reason why changing self-care habits is so challenging, and why efforts often fail. This is especially the case when people are under extreme stress, when cognitive functioning is disrupted and we tend to revert to default habits, whether they are appropriate or not.

More than three quarters of those who are obese, or trying to lose weight, believe their biggest problem is a lack of will power or self-discipline, given their repeated disappointments and failures. In other words, intention is not nearly enough, no matter how important it seems to stay on course. Instead, it is consistent patterns that take over, many of them highly counterproductive. For example, one study compared the ways that normal weight and obese individuals operated at all-you-can-eat buffets (Wansink & Payne, 2008). There were distinct, quite interesting differences in their behavior. Normal weight individuals tended to choose seats facing away from the food, often booths out of sight. They typically checked out all the choices ahead of time before grabbing a plate. They preferred booths over chairs, and routinely put napkins on their laps, all of which made it more difficult for them to go back for multiple helpings. By contrast, obese people started at the front of the buffet line, neglecting to get an overview of what was available before they dipped in. They chose chairs facing the food for easy access—and consistent visual trigger cues. They were thus much less intentional and selective in their choices.

This example also suggests how better self-care habits can be established by disrupting the automatic chain of action in which certain undesirable behaviors continue in spite of one's intentions. The brain may love habit formation to save time and energy but it often fails to recognize when automatic choices are not in the best interest of our health and well-being. If those with weight difficulties really wanted to have greater success, it isn't diets that are necessarily the answer as much as altering patterns of routine behavior. With respect to eating behavior, for example, breaking the habit chain involves choosing an inside seat in a booth far away from the buffet line, and making a choice to survey options before making selections. Instead of mindlessly going through the buffet in the usual pattern, the person would reflect on guiding questions: "Which is the more healthy option?" "What did I already eat for breakfast?" "What would I typically pick, and what could I do differently?" "Which choice will satisfy me the most now, and later?"

As mentioned, because entrenched habits are so strongly reinforced over time, they never really become completely erased, leading to relapses quite easily even after new, more functional habits have been introduced as alternatives. This suggests how truly difficult it is to form relatively permanent self-care habits such as regular exercise: It can take anywhere from three weeks to 250 consecutive days before a simple health behavior like walking after dinner or going to the gym becomes automatic and habituated (Kaushal & Rhodes, 2015).

Habitual Dysfunctional Thinking

We are often witnesses to some of the cognitive habits that so dominate our clients' behavior and choices, patterns that ensure continued difficulties in spite of best intentions. People tell themselves all kinds of things that are not in their best interests, persisting in these beliefs because they are familiar and, in their own way, somewhat comfortable. Common examples we hear all the time reflect themes such as the following: "I'm not the sort of person who does that kind of thing," or "It's not my fault this happens all the time," or "I've always been this way," or "I can't help it," or other forms of externalized, helpless thinking.

We do our very best to challenge some of these assumptions and internalized habits but often with a sense of futility. Sometimes it feels like we are just talking to ourselves since these admonishments often seem to make very little dent in behavior. At least one of the benefits of helping others is that we can't help but internalize some of the things we say in session. It is natural over time that we are inclined to tell ourselves many of the same things we offer to clients when we remind them they are exaggerating, distorting, or otherwise thinking quite unreasonably. And yet we are also prone to lapse into the same kinds of cognitive distortions that afflict those we assist. The things we tell ourselves about our predicament determine, to a large degree, how we feel about our work and whether we see ourselves as heroines, survivors, or victims.

Overthinking, in many ways, can also inhibit new habit formation. The more you question, reflect, consider, explore, the more likely you will be to postpone action for a little bit, missing the "sweet spot" for grooving neurons in the brain during the 60 seconds or so when it is most amenable to reprogramming. The chain of automatic behavior is broken once you wonder, "What if … ?" "What would happen … ?" "Why was I … ?" "I'm not sure if … ?" Habits form once we stop planning and preparing and simply allow for the natural programming to occur.

Depending on one's preferred theoretical orientation and therapeutic approach, recognizable dysfunctional cognitive patterns may be in evidence, leading to complacency, procrastination, or inaction. Regardless of the labels and terms employed, almost every therapeutic approach challenges thinking that sabotages change efforts, whether it is called reframing, looking for exceptions, disputing irrational beliefs, identifying cognitive distortions, and so on. Examples include some of the following:

> **Polarized thinking.** Everything is conceptualized as black or white, good or bad, success or failure, limiting the subtleties, complexities, and gray areas that don't so much define, as describe, actions in extreme terms. Clients use terms like "never" and "always" to describe their behavior, hardly accurate and realistic accounts of behavior that are manifested most often along a continuum.

> **Catastrophizing.** These are exaggerations that imagine the absolute worst that can happen. This sort of thinking is disturbing enough but is often followed by overgeneralizing thoughts to focus only on the possible negative outcomes.

Overattachment. This refers to insisting on illusions of fairness and a just world, that you get what you deserve, that bullies and abusers are punished, that you will always be appropriately appreciated and recognized. Alas, the world is hardly constructed that way, since some people play by very different rules that permit deception, manipulation, exploitation, marginalization, and domination.

Over-personalizing. This involves accepting *way* too much responsibility for certain stressful situations. Given that problems or disappointments at work are usually impacted significantly by systemic factors, it is hardly realistic and accurate to hold beliefs that everyone is out to get you (unless they really are).

Externalizing blame. This is the opposite exaggeration of the previous one, refusing to accept any responsibility for events or outcomes, blaming clients for being uncooperative or extraneous variables that may indeed be operating.

There are so many other varieties of dysfunctional, self-defeating thought patterns that are mentioned as part of different therapeutic approaches, but what they all suggest is that the best way to alter bad habits is to begin with the internal processing that legitimizes this behavior.

Habits as Rituals

Another way to view habits is that they can take the form of soothing, self-care rituals, especially during times of uncertainty or feeling out of control. They exist in all cultures, whether in the form of prayer, affirmations, or social connections. Children recite the Pledge of Allegiance before school begins, or say grace before a meal begins. Shaking hands, celebrating birthdays, knocking on wood, attending ceremonies, and reciting incantations are all common examples. Sometimes they even develop into superstitious beliefs, which is not surprising considering that 80% of professional athletes admit to some particular stress-reducing ritual they engage in related to their sport. Golfer Tiger Woods insisted on wearing red shirts to empower his performance. Tennis champion Serena Williams never changes her smelly socks once a tournament begins. There are some really weird ones, too. Baseball player Jason Giambi would wear a gold thong for underwear to get out of a batting slump. Relief pitcher Turk Wendell was a full-blown maniac when it came to his self-care rituals, insisting that umpires roll rather than throw the ball back to him and drawing three crosses in the dirt in front of the pitching mound. He also brushed his teeth in between each inning and wore a special necklace adorned with the teeth and claws of the animals he had hunted. Baseball player Moises Alou urinated on his hands to toughen them up, but that was still not as peculiar as mixed martial artist Lyoto Machida who insisted on *drinking* his urine before a fight. Basketball players are known to do all kinds of unusual things before shooting free throws—mumbling to themselves, dribbling the ball a certain way and number of times, even doing a little jig before launching the ball. All of these patterns have developed as grounding rituals to trigger muscle memory.

Because habitual rituals are internalized, ingrained, automatic, and take place without conscious choice, they are particularly suitable for any lifestyle choices that we may wish to make permanent daily actions. In order for this to occur, however, the behavior must be (or feel) rewarded in a significant way. These feelings of accomplishment or satisfaction are not just experienced as a prize for doing something but also may represent an attempt to ward off negative reactions that could result from complacency. This very moment, as I write these words, I notice that it is long past the usual time in which I would visit the gym or go for a run, a routine that is almost never disrupted no matter what circumstances, obligations, or distractions are present.

It just doesn't feel acceptable to me to skip a day of exercise because of concerns it will compromise my sleep, stress, routines, and sense of well-being. Does this seem compulsive? I readily agree that it certainly qualifies as such, but without apology, since it helps to stabilize my life and my chattering, incessant brain. This is part of what William Glasser (1976) once conceived of as "positive addictions." I recall him once telling me about a case (Kottler & Carlson, 2003), the last patient he ever saw in therapy, in which a young woman had a very peculiar eating disorder: She had this irresistible impulse to eat snacks from decaying garbage cans in the alleys behind the homes of her neighborhood. Although she was from a privileged family in an affluent area, she nevertheless felt compelled to dive into dumpsters, whether as a form of indulgence, acting out, or pathological self-punishment. Her family tried everything to break this habit but without success. Although Glasser, at the time, had ended his clinical practice, he agreed to see her for a brief consultation. Characteristic of his "choice theory" approach, rather than delving into the reasons for this behavior, exploring the meaning and consequences of her choice, Glasser was only interested in substituting this self-destructive habit with a more positive addiction to replace it. He had already surmised that the main reason for this behavior was because it drove the woman's family crazy and she enjoyed this sense of power.

Rather than talking to her in his office, Glasser instead invited her to go for a run with him through the alleys of her neighborhood. "As long as you are going to be addicted to something," he told her, "you might as well pick something that is good for you." They set up a regular time to meet twice a week and would run through the alleys, passing garbage cans along the way, but without giving them much notice. He believed this new self-care habit gave her a different sense of control, one without the disturbing side effects or need to punish others because of feelings of resentment.

Consider why some people exercise daily and habitually without the slightest chance they might lapse or "forget" to do so. It is never surprising why someone would declare the intention to do so, given all the evidence for exercise's benefits, but it is indeed interesting why some are able to persist in the face of distractions, excuses, and reasons to make a different choice on a given day. It turns out that 90% of habitual exercisers report that it is not a choice at all to work out; rather they do so not only because it feels good to them but also because they crave the activity and don't "feel right" if they skip it. It helps them to feel a sense of achievement and grounds them in their daily functioning. Once the usual routines and cues are elicited—signaled by a particular time of day or some repetitive pattern—the brain begins to send out neurochemical reactions that lead to an actual craving to complete the cycle, much like an addiction (Berridge & Kringelbach, 2008; Doweiko, 2019). What appears to be a burden, obligation, or chore to some people feels more like a pleasurable reward and gift to those who have habitualized this behavior.

There are actual similarities in the brain chemistry between healthful exercise habits and various forms of addiction related to smoking, overeating, alcohol and drug use, gambling, shopping, and other such behaviors: all of them lead to cravings that bypass conscious choice. Each of them is also a classically conditioned response to particular cues that trigger the brain to expect a pleasurable or satisfying reward. This leads to the conclusion that if we want to help someone—or ourselves—establish a constructive self-care ritual, this process begins with discovering clear, consistent cues that signal an automatic response. Just as we automatically brush our teeth after awakening, or just before going to bed, it's important that any new habit is programmed in response to a time of day or similar pattern.

Of course it often takes some dramatic, radical, threatening, challenging, or disruptive set of circumstances in life that lead to such enduring commitments. When people experience tragedies, developmental transitions, age-related changes, and other life transformation, they are far more amenable to considering novel self-care practices. It is under such conditions that they are far more likely to be willing to shake things up and invest the hard work in trying something new. This is the exact scenario that leads people to try therapy in the first place, since they've already exhausted all the options within their current repertoire. Since a so-called "bad" or dysfunctional habit can never really be wiped out of the neuropathways of the brain, it must instead be replaced with an alternative craving that is even stronger and more rewarding (Duhigg, 2012).

Earlier, we explored the nature of "keystone" habits," those critical behaviors that lead to a chain of subsequent actions. One example of this ripple effect might include waking up 15 minutes earlier, which leads to feeling less rushed, having more time to strategically plan the day, and creating space for exercise or a longer break during a packed schedule. This small change in habit may seem insignificant, but such adjustments can often lead to much bigger changes. Another example is common among those who begin and sustain a modest exercise program—just walking a few minutes a day to choosing to walk up stairs as a routine instead of taking the elevator. This may lead to greater awareness and concern for other health choices, such as changing one's diet.

When habit reversal strategies are structured in order to change "bad" habits in favor of those that reduce stress and increase satisfaction, they always begin first with identifying the cues or triggers that automatically lead to undesirable behavior. This is standard practice, whether addressing verbal or facial tics, snacking, nail biting, or any other habit (Nissan et al., 2019). According to the "golden rule of habit change," every habit is composed of three components:

1. a trigger, cue, or stimulus that elicits the automatic response;

2. a response, behavior, or pattern that follows; and

3. a reward that reinforces this cycle. (Duhigg, 2018)

The process of altering this habit is initially sparked by increased awareness of exactly what circumstances, events, or situations are most likely to elicit the habit. This is harder than it seems, because it is likely that such self-awareness ended a long time ago, which is what makes it possible to continue the habit in the first place.

Whether we are working with a client attempting to alter a self-defeating behavior that increases stress, or trying to change some pattern in our own work habits, the effort is launched by carefully monitoring what it is that is sparking the automatic chain. For instance, one therapist deals with cancellations or holes in his schedule during the day by checking news online to occupy himself. The result is significant frustration, discouragement, and disillusionment with the state of affairs in the world, the increased violence, racism, political conflicts, and other depressing news. He notices he is inclined to check the news more out of boredom and inactivity than because he has any burning desire at the moment to know what's going on outside his office. If he really cared, he could wait until he got home (which would likely disrupt his sleep) or the next morning.

This therapist realized that there would continue to be times when there would be unanticipated (or even planned) spaces with little to do before the rush and chaos returned. Rather than automatically scrolling through websites, he decided to break the habit by eliciting alternative responses to the situation, and subsequent feelings, by substituting another option. After experimenting with several possibilities he settled on one that seemed most likely to persist because of its convenience, accessibility, and suitability for his interests. It doesn't really matter which choice he made, as long as he disrupted the previous habit with one that produced different outcomes. Ideally, this change can represent a keystone habit that will lead to other alternations in stress responses.

Saying "No!" and Meaning It, Really, Really Meaning It

Perhaps the single most important habit to internalize is absolutely the simplest, even if it is among the most difficult to practice on a regular basis. The main problem with stress is not adding one more thing to the agenda, no matter how healthy and well regarded, but by subtracting as much as possible. That means setting limits—firm, non-negotiable, enforced limits.

Let's face it: we are all proud of our work ethic. We are martyrs and workhorses who have been rewarded and encouraged our whole lives for doing more than expected, more than others could do. The more busy, efficient, and productive we are, the more accolades we collect, the better positioned for advancement and promotions, the more pride we feel. Perhaps, as one psychiatrist (Lakshmin, 2018) points out, the last thing we need is more self-care and instead what we need are clear boundaries. There is real courage associated with saying "no," declining to participate in certain activities, skipping meetings, because others will be disappointed, especially those who have come to depend on your complete willingness to do whatever is asked. She makes the case that this is neither laziness, complacency, nor a moral failing, but rather what real self-care should be about.

Of course the real difficulty isn't just drawing a line in the sand that you won't cross (a substance that is always shifting); it's also sticking with that commitment and enforcing the boundaries as if your life depends on it (which in some ways it does). It's not as if others at work will be pleased and supportive with this new-found discipline, since it also means more work for them, at least for those who enjoy their role as complaining martyrs. As we are well aware, any change that someone makes requires subsequent systemic adaptations, some of which others find bothersome, annoying, or even threatening.

For those in private practice, it is very challenging to turn any new referral away or decline any new business. One's livelihood depends on a steady flow of clients and who knows when the flow might turn to a trickle or disappear altogether. No matter how packed the schedule, there is always a fear that people will stop calling, so it is really hard to ever turn down a new prospect. This is especially the case because referrals seem to come in waves, like any other "retail" service business in which the flow of "customers" is often unpredictable.

Those who work for public agencies or clinics have a different set of pressures related to meeting session quotas established by administrators. One often doesn't have the luxury to decline a new referral because it is beyond one's expertise or doesn't fit conveniently into the schedule. Yet when we consider what's really at stake, one's health, well-being, and the continued viability of this job, it is absolutely imperative that self-care takes the form of setting reasonable limits. If this is unacceptable to the powers in charge, it's time to consider other options that are more respectful and responsive to what can be handled reasonably.

It is understood and acknowledged that wonderful jobs aren't exactly plentiful and easy to secure. It may very well feel to some professionals that they just don't have many other options and are stuck in the present situation. Under such circumstances, there are still small ways that adjustments can be made. And if that isn't sufficient to reduce the pressure then it's time to seriously consider a new or different kind of job.

Personally, I've never been afraid of the unknown and uncertain future as much as I've been terrified with the prospect of leading just a complacent, ordinary life, one marked by doing what is most convenient, comfortable, or accessible. It's easy to settle into routines that, however unsatisfying, are at least familiar. I've listened to myself way too many times telling clients that they've only got one shot at life and that time is our most precious commodity. Every time I make that point to someone I can't help but turn the admonishment toward myself: To what extent am I truly living my life to the fullest, making the most of every opportunity—not just those that happen to come my way but those I can create myself? None of this has ever come easy for me. I've made so many mistakes and had so many disappointments and failures. I've been promised jobs that didn't come through. My first book proposal was rejected by over 60 publishers; I was so proud of my recovery from their refusals to consider my idea that I literally wallpapered a room in my house with the rejection letters. There are so many other times that I've taken risks, proud of the effort, but still disappointed that nothing meaningful resulted from the attempts to make something happen. I draw on these experiences in my clinical and supervisory work, speaking with authority and confidence about the intrinsic value of at least trying to improve situations, even if the efforts eventually proved unsatisfactory. There is something to be said for such persistence, especially when we've reached a level of desperation that affects so many aspects of our life.

Cues, Rewards, Repetition

As previously mentioned, habits are established and maintained through a relatively simple process in which certain behaviors are consistently reinforced by either internal cues or those in the environment. This is just classical conditioning at its most potent. Yet, in order for these effects to endure over time, there has to be sufficient repetition before the habit becomes relatively permanent and stabilized. Ideally, such behavior becomes intrinsically rewarding and satisfying, so much so that it is viewed as "fun" and "pleasurable" rather than just another burden.

It is the flood of dopamine and other hormones that provide the surge of satisfaction that often accompanies vigorous exercise. That's all very lovely indeed that the body has a way to let us know that what we are doing is greatly appreciated, but alas, this dopamine high lasts less than minute, so the timing for habit formation is crucial to make certain the effects last (Shindou et al., 2018). Casinos and gambling operations understand all too well the way this system works, designing their games so there are unexpected, uncertain rewards associated with play. On numerous occasions playing roulette, slot machines, video poker, or blackjack, it feels like you almost-but-not-quite won, which creates an illusion of victory that keeps the habit going. It is the dopamine rush in gambling, or any other habit formation, that encourages us to keep trying over and over even though there is just rare success. Mobile phone behavior is the clearest example of this, considering that people check their phones an average of 80 times each day, about every ten minutes (many twice as often), hoping that someone reached out to them with something important even though the actual reality is that this is relatively rare (Wolfe, 2018).

Nevertheless, there is something reassuring and comforting about the rituals of our daily lives, all of which are grounded in repetition. Whether in the form of prayer, affirmations, or superstitious behavior, they are all designed to help us deal with uncertainties, doubts, confusion, and perceived lack of control. We've explored how many professional athletes, for instance, engage in some superstitious ritual—meaning habits that actually have no truly functional value—that somehow bolster their sense of confidence and reduce stress. Knocking on wood or crossing one's fingers may be common to bring good luck, but some individuals have taken such habits to wild extremes. Singer Taylor Swift is obsessed with the number 13, the day she was born, the day she turned 13. "Every time I've won an award," she disclosed, "I've been seated in either the 13th seat, the 13th row, the 13th section." Writer Charles Dickens insisted that he only sleep facing north (requiring him to carry a compass) in order to foster his creativity. John Steinbeck claimed that his writing ability was bolstered by his consistent use of compulsively sharpened Blackwing 602 pencils. Benjamin Franklin insisted that his "air baths" in front of an open window (instead of hot bath of water) were the best way to begin his workday. Half the population shares such superstitious beliefs that are hardly based on any empirical evidence, even if they provide an illusion of comfort and control. Nevertheless, there is some evidence that self-soothing habits can help people to perform at a higher level, whether those habits actually provide any clear benefit.

Habituation and Complacency

Habit formation may be helpful, efficient, and functional to simplify and automatize our lives, but it is also inclined to keep us stuck in the same ruts, doing the same things the same way because they are familiar and comfortable. This has been described as the "double law of habits," in that repeating the same patterns over and over tends to strengthen the likelihood of that tendency. One example of this occurs during those times when we feel harried and impatient, repeatedly pushing the close-door button on the elevator even though they haven't actually been connected to anything since the American Disability Act to allow enough time for those who require additional accessibility. This kind of habituation stifles reflective thought and intention. It leads to operating on autopilot without consideration of consequences or even the sense of free choice. This is not necessarily a bad thing during times of stress but can otherwise limit far better options.

We are daily witnesses of the ways that our clients feel stuck in some relationships. They feel trapped in their jobs. They are locked into their routines no matter how unsatisfying they might be, and yet also feel helpless to alter these patterns. We are critical of these predicaments in others but all the while we may be disinclined to examine such behavior in our own lives, unwilling to alter patterns that are not in our best interests.

Originally, habits evolved as behavioral traits to increase adaptive actions during dire circumstances. When under threat or in emergency situations there is no time to think or reason: One must act. Thus seeing a predator and immediately throwing a spear is an action that would have been drilled and practiced over and over again to the point that it becomes automatic. Likewise, in contemporary life, averting an accident on the highway through an immediate response has been rehearsed repeatedly.

For those who are in the throes of extreme stress, or experiencing symptoms of burnout in their jobs, one primary reason is that they feel stuck in routines that are wearing them down, many of which could be adjusted or altered with sufficient commitment and decisive actions. But people often complain they just don't have the energy or the drive or the will to follow through consistently.

As a reminder, people erroneously believe that the single most disruptive impediment to their ability to continue healthy and constructive self-care habits is a lack of will power and commitment. They think they just don't have sufficient self-control, motivation, or self-discipline to persist in their efforts, whether this means sticking with a diet or exercise program, or refraining from some bad habit. This, naturally, leads to feelings of discouragement and inadequacy—that they just don't care enough. Such a conclusion seems inevitable considering that something like 90% of efforts to lose weight, stop smoking, reduce stress, or exercise eventually fail (Vohs & Baumeister, 2017). With respect to reducing chronic stress from daily pressures, the prognosis is even more guarded, given all the challenges that persist in spite of personal desires.

As much as we might be inclined to blame ourselves for a lack of focus and determination, in one sense the very need for self-care is a consequence of broken connections. People suffering from burnout and job-related stress feel a lack of connection in so many ways. Typically their relationships with colleagues and clients are unsatisfactory, just as there may be a breach with supervisors or administrators. There is a mismatch between their own values and priorities and some of the policies and procedures within the organization. The professional often feels a disconnection to any sense of meaning. It feels like little is being accomplished and the person may even begin questioning essential competence. This kind of existential crisis feels like a loss of connection to the original mission of helping people and making a difference in the world. It feels like there is a breach between oneself and the organization, culture, community; tribal affiliations have unraveled. In many cases the intimacy with family, friends, and loved ones has eroded. They feel lost.

There is no shame in feeling lost at times. Some of our best travel experiences and adventures in life have taken place during those times when we are disoriented and stressed, when we find ourselves in unfamiliar situations and novel environments. Some of our most interesting sessions involve delving into issues and areas that feel fresh and unrehearsed. There are actually advantages to acknowledging, even embracing, our "lostness" when there is the opportunity for further learning, growth, and constructive changes that energize our work and make our lives more fulfilling, stimulating, and exciting.

CHAPTER 9

Appreciating the Joys and Benefits of Service

There's some question, whether a psychotherapist, counselor, teacher, physician, nurse, or member of the clergy, is truly just a job or whether it is a calling. Certainly for many people it sure feels like a job, with all the accompanying drudgery, obligations, responsibilities, and pressures that they may wish to avoid, or at least reduce. Perhaps some professionals would never show up for work again if they didn't have to do so for personal survival and economic realities.

There are those who are driven by the pursuit of fame, wealth, and recognition, but most professionals devote their lives to serving others for additional reasons. We define ourselves in terms of the difference we make in others' lives. We accept far more modest compensation and benefits than if we had chosen to become agents of commerce and industry. We labor under limited resources and less than luxurious conditions. But the rewards we do receive usually compensate for these other frustrations and disappointments.

It is certainly the case that we might complain at times, feel underappreciated, even seriously consider abandoning this career path, but there are few other missions in life that feel as rewarding. There is all kinds of evidence that income and material possessions beyond a moderate level don't appreciably make much difference in terms of life satisfaction and sense of well-being. People may buy lottery tickets hoping to hit the jackpot but those who win often regret the changes that took place afterwards. The same could be said for those who change jobs or careers solely for reasons of financial gain.

You'd be hard-pressed to think of another form of work in which we are not only encouraged, but virtually mandated, to continually work on our own personal growth. Every day we can't help but consider the underlying meaning of our own (and others') behavior, search for deeper purpose in life's journey, develop more satisfying interpersonal engagement in all our relationships, fight injustices, advocate on behalf of the dispossessed and suffering, plus attempt (and partially succeed) in our own modest ways, to change the world.

Most significantly of all, following in the footsteps of the significant historical figures we most admire, we allow our lives to stand as examples of what we value most. I am constantly reminded of the story about Mahatma Gandhi who, during the height of his fame, was pestered by his fans as his notoriety spread around the world. Here is a man, a folk hero, who literally starved himself half to death in order to fight for the independence of his nation and advocate on behalf of his people. He certainly had his own problems and demons, not to mention personal failings, but he nevertheless truly tried to become a model for his followers.

There was once a time when he was about to board a train, on his way to the innumerable crowds waiting for him at the next stop. Reporters and well-wishers badgered him constantly for sage wisdom and advice. One such man rushed up to him just as he was climbing up the steps of the train car to ask him for a spiritual message. Although rushed and distracted, Gandhi patiently smiled at the man, nodded his head, took out a small piece of paper, wrote something on it, folded it, and placed in the man's outstretched hand. After the train departed, the man opened the paper to find written on it, "My life is message."

Gandhi tried his very best to live up to this credo that ruled his life, even with his many failings—sexual improprieties, occasional dishonesty and manipulations, peculiar ideas related to food and sleep, to mention a few. But this principle of living what we teach to others can be the defining feature of our own journey as professional helpers. Unlike Gandhi, who pretended to live as a saint even if his behavior was sometimes less than admirable, most of us have learned to accept our fallible humanness, not as an excuse, but as representative of our intended authenticity, genuineness, and self-acceptance. It is not just by presenting ourselves as objects of perfection and complete competence that we inspire others, but rather by being willing to own our limitations and weaknesses, and demonstrate how committed we are to improving them. We are works in progress in the best sense of what that means: We are continuously working on ourselves to become more effective in what we do, but also better at what we wish to become.

The Gifts of Adversity

During the early morning of March 6, 1987, the passenger ferry HMS *Herald of Free Enterprise* left port in Belgium to cross the English Channel. One of the crew members negligently left the bow door open, resulting in the ship being flooded with sea water within seconds. Almost half of the 459 passengers drowned in the accident, making it one of the worst maritime disasters in history. Most of the passengers had been lounging in the lower decks when, all of a sudden, they found themselves swimming for their lives in freezing water. Many of them lost family members and friends in the tragedy, after which they had to deal with the devastating trauma.

A team of psychologists was recruited to provide support and treatment for the survivors, many of whom were unexpectedly experiencing major difficulties after the incident. Some of them were severely depressed, even feeling suicidal with survivor's guilt; others became highly anxious, presenting symptoms of posttraumatic stress. Sometime after treatment had been administered to those who requested it, a study was undertaken to assess the ongoing effects and lingering symptoms of the survivors (Dalgleish et al., 2000). Approximately 100 of them agreed to be interviewed to talk about their experiences. The researchers discovered that indeed about one third of those they talked to were still reporting symptoms of depression and anxiety. This wasn't much of a surprise. Neither were the reports that less than a third of the interviewees had simply moved on with their lives: It had been a terrible experience but one they would just prefer to forget. But what absolutely astounded the psychologists was that 43% of the survivors said that they now had a significantly improved outlook on life! They found that many of their most intimate relationships had improved. They no longer took things for granted. Many of their life goals had crystalized. Nine out of ten of them said that as a result of the traumatic experience they were willing to engage more fully in their daily activities. It would appear that there was compelling evidence that traumatic events and challenging life circumstance can be for better or worse.

Potential Benefits of Stress

Kelly McGonigal (2016), a noted writer on the upside and benefits of stress, reports a similar study that was completed by researchers at a trauma center after major traffic accidents. They were interested in being able to anticipate who among the victims would be at greatest risk for developing posttraumatic stress disorder. Immediately after the accident they took urine samples of the survivors to measure their levels of stress hormones, and then assessed them one month later to discover that the vast majority (80%) demonstrated resilience and successful recovery from the incidents. Interestingly, they were also the ones who had the highest levels of cortisol and adrenaline in their systems after the accidents, which McGonigal contends is an example of the functional benefits of stress reactions to help with adaption after crises. She reports other examples of how a moderate dose of stress hormones not only helps with recovery, but also enables us to perform at our best, providing boosts of energy, narrowed focus, high motivation, and optimal physical resources.

There is a marked difference, of course, between an actual "threat response" that jeopardizes safety, and a "challenge" response in which we rise to the occasion. During the former, especially when the threat is imagined or exaggerated, stress hormones not only become ramped up but stay at those levels beyond where they are in any way helpful. During a perceived challenge response, determined mostly by what we tell ourselves about the situation and the belief that we have adequate resources to deal with it, the accompanying anxiety is experienced mostly as excitement and interesting stimulation. All of that is predicated on the idea that you have the confidence and skills to handle what comes your way.

The posttraumatic growth movement, led by researchers such as Stephen Joseph, Richard Tedeschi, Lawrence Calhoun, and others, forever changed the ways we view traumatic and stressful experiences. Whereas once upon a time we might give to clients or patients who presented trauma the empathic response, "Oh my gosh! That must be so difficult for you! What a terrible predicament and I can understand why you might feel so depressed and traumatized."

But of course that is an assumption that may not necessarily be valid for everyone. It has now been discovered that there is an expected "one-third rule" in which some people become incapacitated, another third recover reasonably well, and another third experience incredible growth, learning, and gifts as a result of what they lived through.

Attitude and Beliefs Are (Almost) Everything

We are already well aware that, when facing any kind of adversity, one's attitudes, beliefs, and interpretation of the experience determine the ways we metabolize the difficulty, as well as respond to it effectively. Much of the research on stress over the years has been somewhat misleading in that it implies that during times of personal challenge and high emotional arousal, even a certain amount of apprehension and anxiety, we are risking our long-term health and even increasing the chances of premature death from heart disease, stroke, and cancer. It is certainly the case that chronic, persistent, extreme stress can produce major deleterious symptoms as a direct result of flooding hormonal responses that overreact and misinterpret potential threats and dangers. What is less known is that these effects are impacted, for better or worse, by our beliefs about stress as potentially harmful or relatively benign. There is some compelling evidence that those who believe their stress and anxiety are dangerous to their well-being are actually increasing their suffering and potential harm (McGonigal, 2016). Likewise, those who interpret their stressful experiences as exciting, stimulating, and growth-oriented are likely to avoid many of the negative effects. If you are convinced that stress is really bad for you, there is a significantly greater likelihood this will be the case (Fischer et al., 2016).

In one review of how superstar performers manage their own stress under extraordinarily pressured situations, some clues are revealed about the ways that one's attitude so shapes optimal responses (Sands, 2019). Astronaut John Glenn, the first to orbit the Earth, revealed that it was his own extraordinary preparation and complete knowledge of every possible scenario that created a kind of "constructive apprehension," a state he considered "the best antidote to fear." An 8th-grade spelling bee champion maintains her composure by focusing on all the support of her friends and family in the audience, drawing strength under pressure. Celebrity talk show host Oprah Winfrey reduces the anxiety she feels by accepting what is present rather than what she wants and expects. French daredevil Philippe Petit, who famously walked across a tightrope connecting the Twin Towers of the World Trade Center in 1974, perhaps the most stressful act imaginable, revealed, "A clever tool in the arsenal to destroy fear: If a nightmare taps you on the shoulder, do not turn around immediately expecting to be scared." In other words, he didn't allow himself to acknowledge fear and anxiety since he remained so focused on the death-defying task at hand. Gymnastics star Simone Biles takes an opposite tack from most others, a strategy that works for her, in which she tries not to overthink or over-focus on an upcoming event, instead allowing herself to become distracted by the people in attendance. "I guess I'm just different," she says, but what she really means is that she discovered an individualized routine to deal with stress that works best for her.

Any life change, transition, or perceived traumatic experience is certainly disruptive in many ways. They create conditions of uncertainty, doubt, and emotional upheaval. But they also represent opportunities for tremendous learning and growth. Relocations, job changes, divorce, rejection, aging, losses, adventure, financial difficulties, and disabilities all have one thing in common: They require a degree of adaptation and adjustment. Under such circumstances, you are not only permitted, but required, to break from previous patterns and try something quite different.

Under stressful, overwhelming circumstances, we tend to fall back on previous habits and coping strategies, whether they are appropriate or not. Habits were specifically designed for such situations when cognitive clarity is muddled. That's why athletes and performers are drilled constantly on those skill sets that will respond automatically and instantaneously when they appear to be needed. It's also why we persist in responding in certain ways to frustrating experiences even though it's pretty clear that those choices are not working very well. You honk your horn in rush hour traffic even though such gestures are futile. And the most dysfunctional habits of all often relate to relational conflict: An adolescent doesn't comply with parental expectations, so her mother yells at her to clean her room. She becomes even more defiant, so the mother yells even louder. This enrages the girl, who begins screaming back at her mother, triggering further escalation of what was originally just a mild annoyance—all because of an automatic response. Yet such conflicts also provide opportunities for changing the patterns—if you are paying close attention to them and their consequences.

Searching for the Gifts of Adversity

As mentioned earlier, it used to be the case that when a client shared a story that featured some trauma, disaster, or disappointment, we would automatically reply with the empathic response, "Oh my gosh, that must have been so terrible for you!"

It wasn't until someone contradicted me that I realized I had jumped to my own conclusions and projected my own feelings of helplessness onto the situation: "Well, ah, no, not really. I mean, yeah it was a difficult situation but really not that bad. Not a big deal. I actually feel grateful in some ways about what happened in that it taught me some important lessons."

I was inclined to interpret this response as disengagement from the experience and denial of feelings, challenging the person to explore more deeply into so-called repressed emotions that were clearly being swept under the rug. But now we realize, of course, that people respond to adversity in a multitude of different ways, and some people fall clearly into groups that recover quite quickly, or even feel grateful for the transformations that take place afterward.

When people are asked to think of an extremely stressful and difficult predicament in their lives, they often immediately point to some situation in which there was considerable suffering and life disruption. But when they are asked to focus on the benefits, growth, and lessons learned after the difficulty, and then to share these insights in a journal or with others in a group, they show much less tension, physiological arousal, and negative moods. They report feeling more control and much greater gratitude (McCullough et al., 2006; Rosenthal, 2013).

It is precisely the challenges of life's difficulties and overcoming adversity that leads to greater resources, hardiness, and resilience in the workplace, what has been referred to as "psychological capital" that protects and empowers us during unpredictable challenges, whether they involve frustrations with difficult clients or colleagues (Youssef-Morgan & Petersen, 2019).

Hugs Really Do Help

Stress is just another way to focus our attention on things that we are ignoring. In addition to all the hundreds of techniques, methods, strategies, tools, apps, programs, and classes designed to reduce overwhelming symptoms, it is the simplest and most obvious solution that is optimally effective. The single most useful means to cope with stress, besides setting limits, involves increased social support and intimate connections to others. We are just not meant to handle such things on our own, in spite of the emphasis on independence, autonomy, and self-sufficiency in our culture.

During the COVID-19 pandemic when people were forced into isolation and social distancing, one of the greatest challenges was meeting the hunger for intimate contact with others. There is only so much satisfaction in this realm that can be met through video conferencing. People require close, physical contact in order to function well as a community. Our species is, by definition, a "social animal," meaning that our continued survival has always depended on our ability and commitment to closely coordinate our actions, support one another, and cooperate effectively. This is how we managed to gather and hunt food, as well as protect ourselves in ancient days, in spite of our lack of protective armor, claws and sharp teeth, and blazing speed. This has no less been true in more contemporary life in which our productivity, wellbeing, and security are very much related to how well we remain connected to others.

The human body was constructed with systems in place that are designed to deal with challenging situations we might face. The "fight or flight" reaction is one such example that purports to prepare the body for self-protection by mobilizing every system to increase stamina, strength, and visual acuity and shutting down any extraneous system that will not be needed during the emergency, thereby hoarding energy and fuel. The sympathetic nervous system and endocrine system work in concert to boost heart rate, respiration, and other responses that are optimal during crises. The problem, of course, is when these systems overreact or don't turn off once the perceived danger is over.

Whereas stimulating hormones like adrenaline, cortisol, or epinephrine speed up our systems, the pituitary gland also releases oxytocin to help with recovery. There is nothing more reliable to trigger this endocrine response than a simple hug or some other form of social bonding. This is the case with most animals as it is with humans. It also explains why there is such an irresistible urge to complain to colleagues about frustrations and disappointments as a means of recruiting support. It is not that complaining works very well, and it usually makes things feel worse as it creates collective victims, but it helps to address the feelings of isolation and aloneness. This is one reason why during the pandemic pollsters were shocked by how often respondents wouldn't stop talking on the phone about their thoughts and feelings on issues, mostly because they were so desperate to be heard and understood by *anyone*.

Joys, Benefits, and Gifts of Serving Others

We know from all kinds of studies and investigations that people involved in selfless, altruistic acts of service enjoy several benefits that include a greater sense of well-being and life satisfaction, a much broader worldview and perspective regarding oneself and one's place in the world, and a kind of spiritual transcendence at times that leads to a renewed sense of faith. There is a distinct feeling of leaving a legacy from one's professional work, one that helped make the world a better place in some modest ways. There is even considerable evidence that Nature rewards altruism and advocacy for the good of the community, leading to an increased lifespan, an immunity to disease, and reduced chronic pain. There are measurable surges of oxytocin and vasopressin, known as the "helper's high"—evolution's gift for selfless service (Bea, 2016; Dossey, 2018). Then there are also far more personal rewards that result in feelings of redemption that our own life challenges and suffering help us to make a difference in others' lives. This is far more than just earning a ticket to heaven and helps to create a sense of meaning and purpose.

For those of us who help for a living, even if we are well compensated for our efforts, there are also distinct joys and rewards from this work, often acknowledged if not regularly recognized and celebrated (Kottler, 2017, 2018; Kottler & Carlson, 2015; Kottler et al., 2013; Kottler & Safari, 2019; Norcross & Vanden-Bos, 2018; Skovholt & Trotter-Mathison, 2016). One study interviewed mental health professionals who admitted to significant symptoms of stress on the job, including acute symptoms of vicarious or secondary trauma, and yet all of the practitioners admitted that, in spite of their sacrifices that resulted in severe anxiety, uncertainty, and doubt at times, they still absolutely *loved* their work and wouldn't trade it for anything else (Sawicki, 2019). It is such reminders of what we gain that helps to compensate for the price we sometimes pay in terms of collateral damage, vicarious trauma, and compassion fatigue.

Parallel Process

It has long been known that the changes, impacts, and interpersonal influences in *any* relationship travel in both directions. Although we are charged with the responsibility to promote desired transformations in our clients, we are hardly insulated from their multitudinous effects on us. Although this is often discussed in the literature as undesirable countertransference or projective identification reactions, just as often there is subtle, unconscious, and sometimes direct impact that provides us with our own opportunities to reflect on the directions of our lives. So often when we find ourselves telling clients what to do to improve their lives we find that we are also talking to ourselves. What other job in the world provides this sort of ongoing incentive to continue our own growth, learning, and development in such a focused, natural way? There is, in fact, no other profession in which everything we learn in our work makes us a better person, and everything we learn in life makes us more skilled as practitioners of our craft.

There isn't a day that goes by that we don't learn something remarkable about ourselves as a result of the intense, intimate conversations we have with our clients. They challenge us in ways that test our patience. They push us to consider subjects that are rarely disclosed aloud. It is virtually impossible to close our ears, or our hearts, to the powerful stories that are shared with us.

Wisdom

Essentially, what we do for a living is collect the most useful knowledge that can be applied to personal problem solving and help others to internalize these ideas to improve their lives. There are significant, meaningful lessons that accrue for those of us who explore deeply the ultimate meaning of a well-lived life. We are the designated sages and gurus of contemporary life that is so dominated by superficial, quick fixes; Google searches; and simplistic answers. The wisdom we hold was attained through considerable effort and dedicated commitment. Although it was developed primarily to help others we can't help but apply such hard-won insights to ourselves, promoting a degree of self-awareness and enlightenment that is somewhat rare among our species.

We read widely, always searching for new ways to make sense of behavior. We constantly reflect on the meaning of others' actions, improving the breadth of our knowledge about the human condition. We walk through life scanning, searching, exploring, exquisitely sensitive and attuned to everything around us. And it is from such dedicated commitment to learning and growth that we are respected and consulted for the most important questions in life.

Drama

This is a favorite of mine, particularly because I am always searching for an antidote to boredom, predictability, and complacency, which I associate with a kind of sleepwalking through life. As much as I might complain about the burdens that clients bring to sessions, I am fascinated and riveted by their stories that feature so much tragedy, conflict, and, at times, comic relief. It is absolutely astounding the extent to which people will engage in the most extraordinarily self-defeating, self-destructive, self-sabotaging behaviors. We are witnesses, voyeurs in a sense, to plotlines that can't be rivaled by the most sad and disturbing shows or films on the screen. And yet we are hardly passive viewers in these narratives, empowered and deputized as we are to alter the trajectory of the action, writing new scenes for enactment, directing the protagonist to continue the noble quest toward a self-determined Holy Grail.

The tales that clients bring to us each day are filled with dramatic episodes of courage or terror, resilience or trauma, the plotlines revealing aspects of human behavior that are astounding in their self-destructiveness. We may maintain a neutral voice and straight face during some client disclosures but inside we are sometimes screaming in horror, frustration, or fascination at how misguided people can be in the choices they make.

Playing Detective

This may not so much be a reward as it is an integral part of the job we enjoy most. We solve mysteries. We uncover secrets. We attempt to make sense of chaos and confusion. We doggedly pursue lines of inquiry that have long been denied or ignored. We unravel the threads of themes from the past, making connections to issues in the present. Sometimes we even identify an essential truth, not only for our clients but for ourselves.

Clients tell us that they are feeling terribly anxious almost all the time and feel absolutely helpless to do much about this condition. They've tried various medications, all without much lasting effect. They have no clue why these feelings take over their lives, why they can't maintain a semblance of control. In response to every question we ask, they just shrug in confusion, or perhaps indifference. Why, they beseech us, do they have these problems and what should they do about them?

Much of the time we have no idea. After all, we just met them. We are flooded with possibilities. We quickly run through a diagnostic decision tree, checking off symptoms that match a particular diagnosis. When did the problems begin? When do the symptoms seem to disappear? What appear to be the triggers? What has worked in the past to reduce their intensity? When all is said and done we are operating like investigators, narrowing the possibilities, forming hypotheses to be tested, attempting to solve the mystery and assemble a complicated puzzle with half the pieces missing.

Intimacy

This is both our greatest scourge and the source of so much joy and satisfaction. We are given free license to engage people in conversation and deep exploration of their most tender, vulnerable, and frightening issues. Therapy sessions are one of the few outlets remaining in contemporary life that are considered so sacred they are not interrupted by messaging, distractions, or other intrusions. All our attention, energy, and focus are directed exclusively toward one, and only one, outlet—and that is to listen carefully, deeply, analytically, and compassionately to our clients' personal disclosures. There are likely few other opportunities in any of our lives in which we are willing to make such a commitment. It is no wonder, then, that some of the most intimate, precious conversations we will ever have in life occur with some of our clients. We are so privileged to earn this trust, even if at times we must shoulder the weight of others' misery.

Based on this sample of benefits, it is clear that one of the best ways to reduce the pressure and burdens that deplete our energy is to be reminded that there is a balance to be maintained. Just as we teach others to change their attitudes toward perceived annoyances, so too do we transform our own interpretations of what may previously have felt troublesome but is actually just part of this journey we have chosen for ourselves.

There are so many other gifts, joys, and benefits that are part of the healer's journey, since the nature of our work requires so much self-reflection and self-scrutiny. We are continuously upgrading our skill set, adding to our repertoire, improving our interpersonal sensitivity, increasing our knowledge, learning new strategies and ways of thinking about difficulties. We are continuously tested and pushed to consider possibilities that have never occurred to us previously.

Yes, it is true that our own unresolved personal issues are frequently triggered, our greatest fears revealed, our uncertainties brought to light. This is our burden but also presents so many opportunities to work on ourselves, modeling for our clients a deep commitment to ongoing self-care. Since any activity, exercise, or behavior that we wish to sustain over time must feel rewarding and satisfying in some way, it is crucial that we fully recognize, acknowledge, and honor the satisfaction, pride, sense of achievement, even joy, in doing things that may have previously seemed burdensome. It is also just as important that we fully recognize and embrace our own limitations, lapses, and shortcomings, modeling such self-forgiveness for those we help.

Empathy for Others, Compassion for Self

Self-compassion has been described as the internal process of treating oneself with kindness, understanding, and forgiveness for one's lapses, mistakes, and failures (Bluth & Neff, 2018). It has been found to significantly reduce stress as well as to encourage better compliance with self-care strategies and health-promoting behavior. It operates primarily by fostering greater patience and reducing self-criticism, recognizing the intrinsic nature of our imperfect selves, and providing reminders to not overidentify with struggles but rather see them as part of a balanced life.

Even though there is considerable evidence that self-compassion is generally viewed as a good thing, most of us still don't understand how and why it works so well to mediate stress challenges at work and in life. What is clear is that those professionals who practice greater kindness and forgiveness of one's mistakes tend to engage in much more healthy behavior with regard to self-care efforts, including (a) healthier eating, (b) more regular exercise, (c) less likelihood of smoking, and (d) more compliance with medical advice. In addition, it's been found that such an attitude contributes to greater self-regulation of emotion in general and a better ability to recover from disappointments (Homan & Sirois, 2017).

With respect to so-called compassion fatigue, also associated with vicarious trauma, and secondary trauma, the term is a bit of a misnomer, since it is really empathy that becomes depleted and creates greater distance with clients. It is actually compassion for oneself that is the cure (Mills & Chapman, 2016). In order to feel true compassion for others, we must first feel some degree of compassion for ourselves. According to the Dalai Lama, "having compassion starts and ends with having compassion for all those unwanted parts of ourselves. The healing comes from letting there be room for all of this to happen: room for grief, for relief, for misery, for joy."

The most accessible, reliable, and effective self-care strategy of all, one that certainly reduces the burdens of responsibilities and obligations, involves simply practicing self-forgiveness. After all, it is the feelings of shame and inadequacy that create so much internal turmoil, at least as much as external pressures. Even just daily reminders to think about personal failings in a less critical and more generous manner makes all the difference, not as an excuse for such weaknesses but as an acceptance of one's humanness (Zhang et al., 2019).

Some Important Reminders of What Therapists Tell Their Clients

Many helping professionals are doing pretty well, considering the nature of their work, the demands on their time, and the realities of their daily lives. In spite of all the attention on the so-called "stress epidemic," the general population is doing okay as well, except for those struggling with depression, anxiety, or chronic pain. Of course that's a pretty big exception, especially for those of us who spend our lives with those people who are struggling the most. It distorts our view of the world in the same way that certain "news" outlets significantly distort the realities of what is actually happening.

Just like our clients, we are hardly helpless victims of circumstances beyond our control. Throughout human history, the most common causes of death were infectious diseases from which we had no protection and cure—cholera, small-pox, influenza, plague, diphtheria, and more recently, coronavirus. Nowadays, summarizes Bryson (2019), in his discussion of mortality, "we live in an age in which we are killed, more often than not, by lifestyle" (p. 368). He is referring, of course, to the choices we make related to the ways we live our lives, and the ways we so ignore our own self-care. Today it is lack of exercise, poor diet, obesity, addictions, risky behavior, car accidents, or suicide that are more likely to kill us. "We are in effect choosing how we shall die, albeit without much reflection or insight."

Psychologists have all but abandoned the study of "happiness," supposedly a stable state that is virtually impossible to maintain every minute in our lives. They've learned that happiness and well-being are not necessarily related to feeling good all the time, since the most satisfying and enjoyable moments in our lives occur when we are doing things that may be stressful and difficult, testing ourselves in some athletic, training, or learning endeavor. It is during times when we feel most useful and competent, regardless of what we are doing and how stressful it might be, that we may feel most satisfied (Weems et al., 2016). That's another reason why *self*-care efforts are so misguided, burdensome, and essentially ineffective, since the longest term boosts to mood occur most often when assisting others in acts of compassion, kindness, or altruism. As we've seen so often, it is precisely the obsession and focus on self that can so often lead to increased misery, pressure, and frustration. We also know that anything we do that keeps us physically active, socially engaged, and grateful for what we already have is going to be most effective in producing feelings of goodwill and satisfaction (Miller et al., 2019). The best news of all is that, given that our work is all about being useful, we are actually in a far better position than others to control the trajectory of our own lives.

Considering that self-care has now become a national obsession, the single most popular kind of mobile app, therapists are going to have to adapt their thinking and methods to capitalize on these preferences. Self-care apps are now a $40 billion industry, with people spending 20% of their disposable income, an average of $200 per month, to treat themselves for stress and emotional discomfort.

Biometric sensors will eventually become commonplace, coupled with sophisticated algorithms, that can accurately read, assess, and analyze not only our precise physiological conditions, but also our most subtle emotions. These sensors will not only be used for identification and security purposes (facial recognition, retinal scans) but also to recognize and identify emotional conditions. Stress levels will be continuously monitored, sending data directly not just to medical specialists but also marketing companies that can more effectively target products and services to the most subtle interests, even those with which you are not yet consciously aware.

In addition, in the aftermath of the coronavirus when telehealth and virtual therapy became the norm for many helping professionals and their clients/patients it is likely that this trend will only continue in the future. Even though few of us have ever received systematic training and supervision in the unique methods and challenges of these delivery systems it is expected that this will become the new normal in many contexts and situations.

How will all of this affect and impact the market for talk therapy, we can justifiably wonder? Will these new technologies increasingly become adjuncts to sessions in which our clients will continuously send reports, behavioral indices, emotion monitors, and other data to us? Will we build interventions and reminders into them to keep clients on course? Will we be replaced altogether by the likes of Alexa or Siri, augmented intelligence devices? If someone is walking around the house and mutters to himself, "I'm depressed," Alexa will immediately reply with, "I'm so sorry to hear you are feeling bad. It's going to get better with time." Such a hopeful message may be a little reassuring but it isn't going to fix whatever is leading to the problems.

It's interesting to consider what the future will bring. Since some of these devices are actually listening and monitoring conversations and goings-on in the home or on your phone, as well as collecting data on everything you post, say, or buy online, it's only a matter of time before they will enter into the dialogue: "Sorry to interrupt your dinner," Alexa might blurt out one evening, "but I couldn't help but hear that you are having a disagreement about who is going to wash the dishes tonight. I understand that you've all had a tough, stressful day. But might I suggest … "

When All Else Fails

If your work is not bringing you joy and satisfaction, if you find yourself dreading the beginning of a new day, if your colleagues are less than supportive and your supervisor isn't much help at all, if it feels like your clients are unappreciative or a pain in the butt, maybe it's time to do something else, or at least do it somewhere else.

Approximately three quarters of the workforce say they feel "disengaged" from their jobs and discouraged by poor morale. They attribute this to a host of factors. They don't feel valued or rewarded for their efforts. They don't feel adequately compensated for their effort and time. They question whether they are really doing anything that matters very much or is making any kind of difference. They don't feel they are growing or learning in their jobs. They may simply not trust the leadership in terms of their goals, priorities, and plans. In each of these cases, people often settle for a degree of mediocrity, telling themselves it's too much trouble to change jobs, or they don't think they can find anything better. And yet this is another one of those instances in which we tell our clients how important it is to take constructive risks and not settle for mere coping, while we may be reluctant to take such actions ourselves when we feel less than satisfied.

I'm not suggesting we necessarily run away from discomforts and dissatisfactions. It is far preferable to work things out where we are, if that is indeed viable. And sometimes it just isn't possible, given the nature of the difficulties on site, or the severity of the problems that don't appear likely to change anytime soon. Sometimes it is better to demonstrate patience and endurance, to wait things out until certain people move on or there are changes in the organizational culture. This is especially true if we want to become fearless models for our clients, willing and able to do the hard things that would make things so much better.

Any life change, whether voluntary or the result of circumstances beyond one's control, are times of uncertainty, instability, stress, and confusion. Whether the result of trauma, divorce, adventure, catastrophe, relocation, illness, financial hardship, or anything else, there is some disruption and instability that almost always leads to some sort of adjustment, if not personal transformation. These can become opportunities to reinvent oneself, to experiment with new ways of being, even to change one's identity.

When it isn't possible—or doesn't feel likely—that relief is only a matter of altering one's attitude toward a situation, it's time to get some help. The most obvious place for that is in counseling, coaching, or therapy to deal with the underlying issues that are getting in the way and recruit support for the changes that must take place. The vast majority of practicing therapists, approaching close to 90%, have at one time or another chosen to seek the services of a colleague (Norcross & Guy, 2005). Those most likely and open to do so tend to be practitioners who have adopted psychodynamic or humanistic approaches, since they tend to emphasize the importance of remaining personally clear. Regardless of the kind of treatment that is selected, and for whatever reasons, 90% of those who sought help reported the experience as helpful and valuable in overcoming difficulties (Orlinsky & Ronnestad, 2005).

What the Future Will Bring

As technological innovations continue to alter the landscape of everyday life in a multitude of ways, we can expect that self-care strategies will become transformed as well into something unrecognizable today. As highlighted previously, biometric data generated from wearable devices, or even implants, will send a flow of information to health professionals, who will be continuously monitoring every system in our bodies, notifying us if there is any anomaly or the presence of even a handful of cancer cells. Sensors will continuously measure blood, respiration, brain activity, gait, moods, as well as responses to everything we encounter during the day, noting internal reactions to any and every stimulus. Artificial intelligence programs will then reliably predict the trajectory of any biological process, perhaps automatically making adjustments in physiological functioning via chemical or other delivery systems.

This might appear to bode well for the future of health, since the earliest signs or symptoms of any problem or disease will be recognized and addressed immediately. However, this will also mean that, more than ever before, we will be scrupulously and obsessively notified and aware of any and all disruptions in the system. In other words, each of us will be "sick" all the time in some way since there will always be something discovered that is not as it could be.

We can also make predictions that, with assistive technology taking care of tasks and jobs that were previously our own responsibility, we may become increasingly complacent, inactive, and sedentary. The major diseases and health problems of today, like obesity, eating disorders, lower back pain, irritable bowel syndrome, drug addictions, depression, and anxiety, are all the result of compromised lifestyle choices. The fears of famine, plague, dysentery, polio, and smallpox have all been replaced with newer, more insidious diseases that result from our own self-neglect.

It's also important to acknowledge that self-care efforts are most often compartmentalized to only one domain of experience, exercise for physical conditioning, massage for physical relaxation, yoga for flexibility, social events for relational support, workshops and seminars for professional development, and so on. Yet in order to maintain optimal functioning in the face of stressful challenges, it's critical to address needs in each of different realms (Butler et al., 2019). Furthermore, self-care strategies are best implemented primarily for prevention rather than remediation of difficulties. For example, once sleep disruption takes hold, every other aspect of daily functioning will be affected, including one's ability to concentrate, make sound decisions, eat healthfully, maintain energy, and retain a sense of personal control.

Self-care really *is* the answer—if the question asked is what prolongs life and guarantees a greater sense of professional achievement and personal sense of well-being. There's overwhelming evidence that people who eat a healthy diet of fruits and vegetables, maintain optimal weight, refrain from smoking or drinking alcohol excessively, and are physically active, reduce their risk of death by 75%. In addition, such a lifestyle screams loudly to all those we help that we live what we advocate for others. We believe so strongly in the power of taking full responsibility for one's health, welfare, and life satisfaction that our talk becomes embodied in our own daily behavior. We walk through life as exemplary models of what we teach to others.

References

Adams, C. (2012, June 8). Are psychotherapists crazy? *Washington City Paper*. https://www.washingtoncitypaper.com/columns/straight-dope/article/13043100/straight-dope-are-psychotherapists-crazy

American Psychological Association. (2018, June 27). Vacation time recharges U.S. workers, but positive effects vanish within days, new survey finds: Less than half of employees encouraged to take time off, have enough employer support to manage work stress. *ScienceDaily*. www.sciencedaily.com/releases/2018/06/180627155634.htm

American Psychological Association. (2019). *Health care, mass shootings, 2020 presidential election causing Americans significant stress, new Stress in America survey finds* [Press release]. https://www.apa.org/news/press/releases/stress/

Amstein, P., Vidal, M., Wells-Federman, C., Morgan, B., & Caudill, M. (2002). From chronic pain patient to peer: Benefits and risks of volunteering. *Pain Management Nursing, 3*(3), 94–103.

Anthony, J. (2019). 7 conclusions from the world's largest teacher burnout survey. *Not Waiting for Superman*. https://notwaitingforsuperman.org/teacher-burnout-statistics/

Archer, A. (2017). Integrity and the value of an integrated self. *Journal of Value Inquiry, 51*(3), 435–454.

Arendt, H. (1963). *On revolution*. Viking.

Bartleby. (2019, January 5). The spy who hired me. *The Economist, 50*, 46.

Bea, S. (2016, November 15). Wanna give? This is your brain on a 'helper's high.' *Cleveland Clinic*. https://health.clevelandclinic.org/why-giving-is-good-for-your-health/

Becker, D. (2013). *One nation under stress: The trouble with stress as an idea*. Oxford University Press.

Berridge, K. C., & Kringelbach, M. L. (2008). Affective neuroscience of pleasure: Reward in humans and animals. *Psychopharmacology, 199*, 457–480.

Bloom, L. B. (2020, January 30). Ranked: The world's 20 most stressed-out cities (the worst in the U.S. will surprise you). *Forbes*. https://www.forbes.com/sites/laurabegleybloom/2020/01/30/ranked-worlds-20-most-stressed-out-cities/#f0b9d9519c1a

Bluth, K., & Neff, K. D. (2018). New frontiers in understanding the benefits of self-compassion. *Self and Identity, 17*, 605–608.

Brehony, K. A. (1999). *Ordinary grace*. Riverhead.

Bressi, S. K., & Vaden, E. R. (2017). Reconsidering self-care. *Clinical Social Work Journal, 45*, 33–38.

Bryson, B. (2019). *The body: A guide for occupants*. Doubleday.

Butler, L. D., Mercer, K. A., McClain-Meeder, K., Horne, D. M., & Dudley, M. (2019). Six domains of self-care: Attending to the whole person. *Journal of Human Behavior in the Social Environment, 29*(1), 107–124.

Ciccolo, J. T., Whitworth, J. W., & Sanaz, N. (2019). Psychological benefits of exercise. In M. H. Anshell, S. Petruzzello, & E. Labbe (Eds.), *APA handbook of exercise psychology* (Vol. 2, pp. 93–108). American Psychological Association.

Colman, D. E., Echon, R., Lemay, M. S., McDonald, J., Smith, K. R., Spencer, J., & Swift, J. K. (2016). Efficacy of self-care for graduate students in professional psychology: A meta-analysis. *Training and Education in Professional Psychology, 10*, 188–197.

Crum, A. J., Akinola, M., Martin, A., & Fath, S. (2017). The role of stress mindset in shaping cognitive, emotional, and physiological responses to challenging and threatening stress. *Anxiety, Stress, & Coping, 30*(4), 379–395.

Dalgleish, T., Joseph, S., & Yule, W. (2000). The Herald of Free Enterprise disaster: Lessons from the first six years. *Behavior Modification, 24*, 673–699.

Dalphon, H. (2019). Self-care techniques for social workers: Achieving an ethical harmony between work and well-being. *Journal of Human Behavior in the Social Environment, 29*(1), 85–95.

Danaher, J. (2018, November 9). *Am I a hypocrite? A philosophical self-assessment. Philosophical Disquisitions.* https://philosophicaldisquisitions.blogspot.com/2018/11/am-i-hypocrite-philosophical-self.html

Dattilio, F. M. (2015). The self-care of psychologists and mental health professionals: A review and practitioner guide. *Australian Psychologist, 50*, 393–399.

Davis, D. M., & Hayes, J. A. (2012). What are the benefits of mindfulness? *Monitor on Psychology, 43*(7), 64.

deBara, D. (2019, March 11). Why self-care is the secret to becoming a productivity power-house. *Trello.* https://blog.trello.com/self-care-for-productivity

DeYoung, P. A. (2015). *Relational psychotherapy: A primer.* Routledge.

Dhabhar, F. S. (2019). The power of positive stress—a complementary commentary. *Stress, 22*(5), 526–529.

Diamond, J. (2005). *Guns, germs, and steel.* W.W. Norton.

Dierdorff, E. C. (2020, January 29). Time management is about more than life hacks. *Harvard Business Review.* https://hbr.org/2020/01/time-management-is-about-more-than-life-hacks

Dimitrios, B., & Konstantinos, V. (2014). Organizational culture and job burnout: A review. *International Journal of Research in Management, 2*(1), 2347–4572.

Dorociak, K. E., Rupert, P. A., & Zahniser, E. (2017). Work life, well-being, and self-care across the professional lifespan of psychologists. *Professional Psychology: Research and Practice, 48*(6), 429–437.

Dossey, L. (2018). The helper's high. *Explore, 14*(6), 393–399.

Doweiko, H. E. (2019). *Concepts of chemical dependency* (10th ed.). Cengage.

Duhigg, C. (2012). *The power of habit.* Random House.

Duhigg, C. (2018, July 8). The golden rule of habit change. *Psych Central.* https://psychcentral.com/blog/the-golden-rule-of-habit-change/

Effron, D. A., Markus, H. R., Jackman, L. L., Muramoto, Y., & Muluk, H. (2018). Hypocrisy and culture: Failing to practice what you preach receives harsher interpersonal reactions in independent (vs. interdependent) cultures. *Journal of Experimental and Social Psychology, 76*, 371–384.

Farber, B. A., & Heifetz, L. J. (1982). The process and dimensions of burnout in psychotherapists. *Professional Psychology, 13*, 293–301.

Figley, C. R. (Ed.). (1995). *Compassion fatigue: Secondary traumatic stress disorders from treating the traumatized.* Brunner/Mazel.

Figley, C. R. (Ed.). (2002). *Treating compassion fatigue.* Routledge.

Fischer, S., Nater, U. M., & Laferton, J. A. (2016). Negative stress beliefs predict somatic symptoms on students under academic pressure. *International Journal of Behavioral Medicine, 23*(6), 746–751.

Flora, C. (2019, June 21). Protect yourself from emotional contagion. *Psychology Today.* https://www.psychologytoday.com/us/articles/201906/protect-yourself-emotional-contagion

Francis, A. L. (2018). The embodied theory of stress: A constructionist perspective on the experience of stress. *Review of General Psychology, 22*(4), 398–405.

Fredrickson, B. L. (2003). The value of positive emotions: The emerging science of positive psychology is coming to understand why it's good to feel good. *American Scientist, 91,* 330–335.

Freudenberger, H. J. (1974). Staff burn-out. *Journal of Social Issues, 30*(1), 159–165.

Gebauer, J., Riketta, M., Broemer, P., & Mai, G. (2008). Pleasure and pressure based prosocial motivation: Divergent relations to subjective well-being. *Journal of Research in Personality, 42,* 399–420.

Geller, S. (2017). *A practical guide to cultivating therapeutic presence.* American Psychological Association.

Glasser, W. (1976). *Positive addiction.* Harper.

Green, E. (2015, June). The hypocrisy of professional ethicists. *The Atlantic.* https://www.theatlantic.com/magazine/archive/2015/06/philosophers-are-hypocrites/392087/

Groopman, M. (2008). *How doctors think.* Houghton Mifflin.

Harari, Y. N. (2018). *21 lesson for the 21st century.* Spiegel & Grau.

Hargrove, M. B., Becker, W. S., & Hargove, D. F. (2015). The HRD eustress model: Generating positive stress with challenging work. *Human Resource Development Review, 14*(3), 279–298.

Hatfield, E., Bensman, L., Thornton, P. D., & Rapson, R. L. (2014). New perspectives on emotional contagion: A review of classic and recent research on facial mimicry and contagion. *Interpersona, 8*(2), 12–19.

Havlin, L. (2019, June 4). Is your self-care practice fueling your burnout? *Dazed Digital.* https://www.dazeddigital.com/beauty/soul/article/44713/1/self-care-practice-fuelling-burnout-capitalism

Heid, M. (2019). Rising to the challenge. In R. Sands (Ed.), *The science of stress* (pp. 10–15). Time.

Homan, K. J., & Sirois, F. M. (2017). Self-compassion and physical health: Exploring the roles of perceived stress and health-promoting behaviors. *Health Psychology Open, 4*(2), 1–9.

Hydon, S., Wong, M., Langley, A. K., Stein, B. D., & Kataoka, S. H. (2015). Preventing secondary traumatic stress in educators. *Child and Adolescent Psychiatric Clinics, 24,* 319–333.

Imber, G. (2011). *Genius on the edge: The bizarre double life of William Steward Halsted.* Kaplan.

Jergensen, K. (2018). Practice what you preach: An exploration of DBT therapists personal skill utilization in burnout prevention. *Clinical Social Work Journal, 46,* 187–199.

Jonas, W. (2019). *Health and self-care: A look inside patient and physician perspectives on self-care.* Samueli Foundation. http://drwaynejonas.com/wp-content/uploads/2019/07/health_and_self-care_report_FNL.pdf

Joshu, E. (2019a). Finding balance. In R. Sands (Ed.), *The science of stress* (pp. 42–47). Time.

Joshu, E. (2019b). The perils of social media. In R. Sands (Ed.), *The science of stress* (pp. 78–79). Time.

Kamin, H. S., & Kertes, D. A. (2017). Cortisol and DHEA in development and psychopathology. *Hormones and Behavior, 89,* 69–85.

Kaushal, N., & Rhodes, R. E. (2015). Exercise habit formation in new gym members: A longitudinal study. *Journal of Behavioral Medicine, 38,* 652–653.

King, N. (2016, December 8). When a psychologist succumbed to stress, he coined the term "burnout." *National Public Radio.* https://www.npr.org/2016/12/08/504864961/when-a-psychologist-succumbed-to-stress-he-coined-the-term-burnout

Kirschenbaum, H. (2008). *The life and work of Carl Rogers.* American Counseling Association.

Kluger, J. (2019). Fight or flight forever. In R. Sands (Ed.), *The science of stress* (pp. 4–7). Time.

Kottler, J. A. (1992a). *Compassionate therapy: Working with difficult clients.* Jossey-Bass.

Kottler, J. A. (1992b). Confronting our own hypocrisy: Being a model for our students and clients. *Journal of Counseling and Development, 70,* 475–476.

Kottler, J. A. (2000). *Doing good: Passion and commitment for helping others.* Routledge.

Kottler, J. A. (2015). *Change: What really makes a difference?* Oxford University Press.

Kottler, J. A. (2017). *Secrets of exceptional counselors.* American Counseling Association.

Kottler, J. A. (2018). *Living and being a therapist: A collection of readings.* Cognella.

Kottler, J. A., & Balkin, R. (2017). *Relationships in counseling and the counselor's life.* American Counseling Association.

Kottler, J. A., & Balkin, R. (2020). *Myths, misconceptions, and invalid assumptions of counseling and psychotherapy.* Oxford University Press.

Kottler, J., & Blau, D. (1989). *The imperfect therapist: Learning from failure in therapeutic practice.* Jossey-Bass.

Kottler, J. A., & Carlson, J. (2002). *Bad therapy: Master therapists share their worst failures.* Routledge.

Kottler, J. A., & Carlson, J. (2003). *The mummy at the dining room table: Eminent therapists reveal their most unusual cases and what they teach us about human behavior.* Jossey-Bass.

Kottler, J. A., & Carlson, J. (2006). *The client who changed me: Stories of therapist personal transformation.* Routledge.

Kottler, J. A., & Carlson, J. (2011). *Duped: Lies and deception in psychotherapy.* Routledge.

Kottler, J. A., & Marriner, M. (2009). *Changing people's lives while transforming your own: Paths to social justice and global human rights.* Wiley.

Kozusznik, M. W., Rodriguez, I., & Peiro, J. M. (2015). Eustress and distress climates in teams: Patterns and outcomes. *International Journal of Stress Management, 22*(1), 1–23.

Krause, L. (2017, November 29). Fight burnout and compassion fatigue with lots of self-care ideas. *ACES Connection.* https://www.acesconnection.com/blog/fight-burnout-and-compassion-fatigue-with-lots-of-self-care-ideas

Krick, A., & Felfe, J. (2019). Who benefits from mindfulness? The moderating role of personality and social norms for the effectiveness on psychological and physiological outcomes among police officers. *Journal of Occupational Health Psychology, 25*(2), 99–112. https://doi.org/10.1037/ocp0000159

Laird, A. K. (2018, July 20). Why your self-care methods aren't working—and how to fix that. *Self.* https://www.self.com/story/why-your-self-care-methods-arent-working

Lakshmin, P. (2018, October 5). We don't need self-care; we need boundaries. *Op-Med.* https://opmed.doximity.com/articles/we-dont-need-self-care-we-need-boundaries-79042584b318?_csrf_attempted=yes

Lally, P., Wardle, J., & Gardner, B. (2011). Experiences of habit formation: A qualitative study. *Psychology, Health, and Medicine, 16*(4), 484–489.

Leder, S. (2019). The sabbath antidote. In R. Sands (Ed.), *The science of stress* (pp. 86–89). Time.

Lee, J., Lim, N., Yang, E., & Lee, M. (2011). Antecedents and consequences of three dimensions of burnout in psychotherapists: A meta-analysis. *Professional Psychology: Research and Practice, 42,* 252–258.

Levy, K. N., Hlay, J. K., Johnson, B. N., & Witmer, C. P. (2019). An attachment theoretical perspective on tend-and-befriend stress reactions. *Evolutionary Psychological Science, 5,* 426–439. https://doi.org/10.1007/s40806-019-00197-x

Lieberman, D. E. (2013). *The story of the human body: Evolution, health, and disease.* Vintage.

Luks, A. (1988). Helper's high: Volunteering makes people feel good, physical and emotionally. *Psychology Today, 22*(10), 34–42.

Marsh, N. (2011). *Fat, forty, and fired.* Andrews McMeel.

Martin, C. (2014, March 14). On hypocrisy. *Harper's Magazine.* https://harpers.org/blog/2014/03/on-hypocrisy/

Maslach, C. (2015). *Burnout: The cost of caring.* Malor Books.

Maslach, C., Schaufeli, W. B., & Leiter, M. P. (2001). Job burnout. *Annual Review of Psychology, 52,* 397–422.

Mavridis, C., Harnkness, S., Super, C. M., & Liu, J. L. (2019). Family workers, stress, and the limits of self-care. *Children and Youth Services Review, 103,* 236–246.

McCormack, H. M., MacIntyre, T. E., O'Shea, D., Herring, M. P., & Campbell, M. J. (2018). The prevalence and cause(s) of burnout among applied psychologists: A systematic review. *Frontiers in Psychology, 9,* 1897.

McCullough, M. E., Lindsey, M. E., Root, M. D., & Cohen, A. D. (2006). Writing about the benefits of an interpersonal transgression facilitates forgiveness. *Journal of Consulting and Clinical Psychology, 74*(5), 887–897.

McGonigal, K. (2016). *The upside of stress.* Penguin.

McGonigal, K. (2019). Embrace the pressure. In R. Sands (Ed.), *The science of stress* (pp. 54–57). Time.

McKinnon, J. (1991). Hypocrisy, with a note on integrity. *American Philosophical Quarterly, 28*(4), 321–330.

Miller, K. J., Mesagno, C., McLaren, S., Grace, F., Yates, M., & Gomez, R. (2019). Exercise, mood, self-efficacy, and social support as predictors of depressive symptoms in older adults: Direct and interaction effects. *Frontiers of Psychology, 10,* 1–11.

Mills, J., & Chapman, M. (2016). Compassion and self-compassion in medicine: Self-care for the caregiver. *Australasian Medical Journal, 9*(5), 87–91.

Monsalve-Reyes, C. S., San Luis-Costas, C., Gómez-Urquiza, J. L., Albendín-García, L., Aguayo, R., & Cañadas-De la Fuente, G. A. (2018). Burnout syndrome and its prevalence in primary care nursing: A systematic review and meta-analysis. *BMC Family Practice, 19,* 59.

Montero-Marin, J., Prado-Abril, J., Piva Demarzo, M. M., Gascon, S., & García-Campayo, J. (2014). Coping with stress and types of burnout: Explanatory power of different coping strategies. *PLOS ONE, 9*(2), e89090.

Moskowitz, C. (2008, October 17). Animals stressed out, too. *Live Science.* https://www.livescience.com/2967-animals-stressed.html

Neace, R., & Kottler, J. (2017). Congruence as self-care: Practicing what we preach. *Counselor Magazine, 18*(3), 27–41.

Neal, D. T., Wood, W., Wu, M., & Kurlander, D. (2011). The pull of the past: When do habits persist despite conflict with motives? *Personality and Social Psychology Bulletin, 37*(11), 1428.

Neo, P. (2020, January 3). I'm a psychologist and here's the biggest mistake I see people make with self-care. *MBG.* https://www.mindbodygreen.com/articles/biggest-self-care-mistakes

Newell, J. M., & Nelson-Gardell, D. (2014). A competency based approach to teaching professional self-care: An ethical consideration for social work educators. *Journal of Social Work Education, 50*, 427–439.

Nickels, N., Kubicki, K., & Maestripieri, D. (2017). Sex differences in the effects of psychosocial stress on cooperative and prosocial behavior: Evidence for flight-or-fight in males and tend-and-befriend in females. *Adaptive Human Behavior and Physiology, 3*(2), 171–183.

Nissan, J. B., Kaergaard, M., Laursen, L., Parner, E., & Thomsen, P. H. (2019). Combined habit reversal training and exposure response prevention in a group setting compared to individual training: A randomized controlled clinical trial. *European Child and Adolescent Psychiatry, 28*(1), 57–68.

Norcross, J. C., & Guy, J. D. (2005). Ten therapists: The process of becoming and being. In W. D. Dryden & L. Spurling (Eds.), *On becoming a psychotherapist* (pp. 215–239). Routledge.

Norcross, J. C., & VandenBos, G. R. (2018). *Leaving it at the office: A guide to psychotherapist self-care* (2nd ed.). Guilford.

Oken, D. (1961). What to tell cancer patients: A study of medical attitudes. *Journal of the American Medical Association, 175*(13), 1120–1128.

Oman, D., Thoresen, C. E., & McMahon, K. (1999). Volunteerism and mortality among community-dwelling elderly. *Journal of Health Psychology, 4*(3), 301–316.

Orlinsky, D. E., & Ronnestad, M. H. (2005). *How psychotherapists develop: A study of therapeutic work and professional growth.* American Psychological Association.

Pope, K. S. (2017). *31 recent meta-analyses on the effects of exercise.* https://kspope.com/ethics/exercise-meta-analyses.php

Pope, K. S., Tabachnick, B. G., & Keith-Spiegel, P. (1987). Ethics of practice: The beliefs and behaviors of psychologists as counselors. *American Psychologist, 42*(11), 993–1006.

Post, S. G. (2005). Altruism, happiness, and health: It's good to be good. *International Journal of Behavioral Medicine, 12*(2), 66–77.

Post, S. G. (2011). *The hidden gifts of helping: How the power of giving, compassion, and hope can get us through hard times.* Jossey-Bass.

Post, S. G. (Ed.). (2007). *Altruism and health: Perspectives from empirical research.* Oxford University Press.

Post, S., & Neimark, J. (2007). *Why good things happen to good people.* Doubleday.

Purser, R. E. (2019, September 16). The dark side of mindfulness we need to wake up to. *Refinery29*. https://www.refinery29.com/en-ca/the-dark-side-of-mindfulness-we-need-to-wake-up-to

Ram Dass & Bush, M. (1992). *Compassion in action*. Bell Tower.

Ramsey, N. (2018, July 23). Headline stress disorder: When breaking news is bad for your health. *Healthline*. https://www.healthline.com/health-news/headline-stress-disorder-when-breaking-news-is-bad-for-health#1

Reith, T. P. (2018). Burnout in United States healthcare professionals: A narrative review. *Cureus, 10*(12), e3681.

Renken, E. (2020, January 23). Most Americans are lonely, and our workplace culture may not be helping. *National Public Radio*. https://www.npr.org/sections/health-shots/2020/01/23/798676465/most-americans-are-lonely-and-our-workplace-culture-may-not-be-helping

Rogers, C. (1961). *On becoming a person*. Houghton-Mifflin.

Rogers, C. R. (1995). *A way of being*. Houghton Mifflin.

Rosenthal, N. E. (2013). *Gifts of adversity: The unexpected benefits of life's setbacks, difficulties, and imperfections*. Perigee.

Rothschild, B., & Rand, M. (2006). *Help for the helper: Self-care strategies for managing burnout and stress*. W.W. Norton.

Rupert, P. A., & Dorociak, K. E. (2019). Self-care, stress, and well-being among practicing psychologists. *Professional Psychology: Research and Practice, 50*(5), 343–350.

Rupert, P. A., Miller, A. O., & Dorociak, K. E. (2015). Preventing burnout: What does the research tell us? *Professional Psychology: Research and Practice, 46*, 168–174.

Saakvitne, K. W., & Pearlman, L. A. (1996). *Transforming the pain: A workbook on vicarious traumatization*. W.W. Norton.

Safari, S., & Kottler, J. (2018). *Above the mountain's shadow: A journey of hope and adventure inspired by the forgotten*. Cognella.

Sands, R. (Ed.). (2019). *The science of stress*. Time.

Sapyta, J., Reimer, M., & Bickman, L. (2005). Feedback to clinicians: Theory, research, and practice. *Journal of Clinical Psychology, 61*(2), 145–153.

Sawicki, S. M. (2019). *Mental health workers' vicarious trauma, secondary traumatic stress, and self-care*. DBC Publishing.

Schneider, L. S. (2019a). The risks and uses of dietary supplements. *The Lancet, 18*(9), 814.

Schneider, M. (2019b, September 24). In a new study, 90 percent of employees admit to feeling burned out. *Inc.* https://www.inc.com/michael-schneider/in-a-new-study-90-percent-of-employees-admit-to-feeling-burned-out-here-are-3-ways-to-successfully-manage-it.html

Scudellari, M. (2015). Science myths that will not die. *Nature, 528*, 322–325.

Shensa, A., Sidani, J. E., Dew, M. A., Escobar-Viera, C. G., & Primack, B. A. (2018). Social media use and depression and anxiety: A cluster analysis. *American Journal of Health Behavior, 42*(2), 116–128.

Shensa, A., Sidani, J. E., Escobar-Viera, C. G., Switzer, G. E., Primack, B. A., & Choukas-Bradley, S. (2020). Emotional support from social media and face-to-face relationships: Associations with depression risk among young adults. *Journal of Affective Disorders, 260*, 38–44.

Shindou, T., Shindou, M., Watanabe, S., & Wickens, J. (2018). A silent eligibility trace enables dopamine-dependent synaptic plasticity for reinforcement learning in mouse striatum. *European Journal of Neuroscience.* Advance online publication. https://doi.org/10.1111/ejn.13921

Silva, C. (2017, June 14). The millennial obsession with self-care. *NPR.* https://www.npr.org/2017/06/04/531051473/the-millennial-obsession-with-self-care

Simionato, G. K., & Simpson, S. (2018). Personal risk factors associated with burnout among psychotherapists: A systematic review of the literature. *Journal of Clinical Psychology, 74*(9), 1431–1456.

Skovholt, T. M., & Trotter-Mathison, M. (2016). *The resilient practitioner: Burnout and compassion fatigue and self-care strategies for the helping professions* (3rd ed.). Routledge.

Slavich, G. (2019). Stressnology: The primitive (and problematic) study of life stress exposure and pressing need for better measurement. *Brain, Behavior, and Immunity, 75,* 3–5.

Statman, M. (1997). Hypocrisy and self-deception. *Philosophical Psychology, 10*(1), 57–75.

Staub, E. (2003). *The psychology of good and evil: Why children, adults, and groups help and harm others.* Cambridge University Press.

Stosny, S. (2017, March 4). Overcoming headline stress disorder. *Psychology Today.* https://www.psychologytoday.com/us/blog/anger-in-the-age-entitlement/201703/overcoming-headline-stress-disorder

Taylor, S. E., Klein, L. C., Lewis, B. P., Gruenewald, T. L., Gurung, R. A. R., & Updegraff, J. A. (2000). Biobehavioral responses to stress in females: Tend-and-befriend, not fight-or-fight. *Psychological Review, 107*(3), 411–429.

Thomas, L. (1975). The health care system. *New England Journal of Medicine, 293,* 1245–1246.

Treadway, D. (2020, February). Our calling: A wounded healer's journey. *Psychotherapy Networker,* 33–35, 58.

Van der Linden, S. (2011, December). The helper's high. *Ode Wire.* http://odewire.com/176916/the-helper's-high.html

Vohs, K. D., & Baumeister, R. F. (Eds.). (2017). *Handbook of self-regulation* (3rd ed.). Guilford.

Volhardt, J. R. (2009). Altruism born of suffering and prosocial behavior following adverse life events: A review and conceptualization. *Social Justice Research, 22,* 53–97.

Walsh, R. (2011). Lifestyle and mental health. *American Psychologist, 66*(7), 579–592.

Wansink, B., & Payne, C. R. (2008). Eating behavior and obesity at Chinese buffets. *Obesity, 16*(8), 1957–1960.

Warneken, F., & Tomasello, M. (2006). Altruistic helping in human infants and young chimpanzees. *Science, 311,* 1301–1303.

Warneken, F., & Tomasello, M. (2009). The roots of human altruism. *British Journal of Psychology, 100,* 455–471.

Weems, C. F., Osofsky, J. D., Osofsky, H. J., King, L. S., Hansel, T. C., & Russell, J. D. (2018). Three-year longitudinal study of perceptions of competence and well-being among youth exposed to disasters. *Applied Developmental Science, 22*(1), 29–42.

Weir, K. (2011). The exercise effect. *Monitor on Psychology, 42*(11), 48.

Winch, G. (2019). How to turn off work thoughts during your free time. *TED.* https://www.ted.com/talks/guy_winch_how_to_turn_off_work_thoughts_during_your_free_time

Wolfe, A. (2018, April 2). Guess how often you check your phone every day. *Journal of Accountancy*. https://www.journalofaccountancy.com/newsletters/2018/apr/how-often-use-phone-every-day.html

Wood, W. (2019). *Good habits, bad habits*. Farrar, Straus and Giroux.

Wood, W., & Runger, D. (2015). Psychology of habit. *Annual Review of Psychology, 67*, 289–314.

World Health Organization. (2020). *Burnout an occupational phenomenon: International Classification of Diseases*. https://www.who.int/mental_health/evidence/burn-out/en/

Wunsch, K., Wurst, R., von Dawans, B., Strahler, J., Kasten, N., & Fuchs, R. (2019). Habitual and acute exercise effects on salivary biomarkers in response to psychosocial stress. *Psychoneuroendocrinology, 106*, 216–225.

Yalom, I. (2002). *The gift of therapy*. HarperCollins.

Yasgur, B.S. (2019). Challenging stigma: Should psychiatrists disclose their own mental illness? *Psychiatry Advisor*. https://www.psychiatryadvisor.com/home/topics/mood-disorders/depressive-disorder/challenging-stigma-should-psychiatrists-disclose-their-own-mental-illness/

Youssef-Morgan, C. M., & Petersen, K. (2019). The benefits of developing psychological capital in the workplace. In R. J. Burke & A. M. Richardson (Eds.), *Creating psychologically healthy workplaces* (pp. 113–132). Edward Elgar.

Zhang, J. W., Chen, S., Tomova Shakur, T. K., Bilgin, B., Chai, W. J., Ramis, T., Shaban-Azad, H., Razavi, P., Nutankumar, T., & Manukyan, A. (2019). A compassionate self is a true self? Self-compassion promotes subjective authenticity. *Personality and Social Psychology Bulletin, 45*(9), 1323–1337.

Index

CPSIA information can be obtained
at www.ICGtesting.com
Printed in the USA
LVHW060905120821
695098LV00003B/16